Like It

WORDS FOR EVERYDAY LIVING

Joseph McCray

ISBN-13: 9780991038626
ISBN-10: 0991038622

Like It

Words for Everyday Living

Acknowledgements

I dedicate this book solely to my son Goshen. I always want you to have your dad's thoughts nearby.

To my wife Shawanda, you have read and heard these words many times.

To my sister Lucy, who I talk with most days of the week.

To all my family and friends be blessed.

To Pastors Kenneth O. Robinson and Lady Lenyar Robinson, your words of life help guide me to fulfill my dreams.

To my Lord and Savior Jesus Christ, you give me purpose.

Contents

Introduction

"Like It" – Words for Everyday Living is a collection of words that I have posted throughout the years that have served as words of inspirations, encouragement, wisdom, and humor. I have collected them and place them in order by the year and month, in which I posted the words.

Read these words all the way through or take time and read a few posts daily for that particular month. I believe you will find these words relevant to everyday living.

As a bonus, you get to check if you like those words for that day and write a comment in the book or rewrite my comment. All entries are my original posts from social media.

CHAPTER 1
January

January 1
2013

Whatever ur new year resolution, make sure to exclude fear.

_____ Like

Comment:

January 2
2012

Should a five year old give a two year time out at Chick - Fila?

_____ Like

Comment:

2013

Lunch packed = no searching for food.

_____ Like

Comment:

2014

You don't have to go around letting people know you know the Word of God, in time we'll see.

_____ Like

Comment:

January 3
2012

Sometimes u have to complete ur goal. No more thinking about it, praying about it or asking people about it.

_____ Like

Comment:

2013

I was reflecting last night, that I wanted more than anything that my son know that I love him. I believe that's God's desire that u know he loves you.

_____ Like

Comment:

2014

My sister Lucille has forged through the storms for decades as a mail carrier and so can I.

_____ Like

Comment:

January 4
2012
When u discover what u supposed to be, the world will be glad n ur enemies will be the ones still trying to figure themselves out.

_____ Like

Comment:

My dream is coming to pass right before my eyes! Hallelujah. I'm about to shout n this house.

_____ Like

Comment:

2014
U don't get things done bc u are lazy or u procrastinate, stop that.

_____ Like

Comment:

January 5
2011
reading some old cards and taking notice of two of my nephews who have such neat handwriting. What happen to me?

_____ Like

Comment:

January 6
2011
If a one year old wakes up, stands at the gate n points to the bathroom, does that mean he wants to go to the bathroom? even if he has a diaper on.

_____ Like

Comment:

2011
Before there was FB, there was the family. We brought over the photos, no uploads. Games we played with each other. Words of wisdom and thoughts we shared face to face. It is my hope that the JJ's family would find some time to send a message or inbox each other in person. Thanks to the founder of this social network, but it's been around for ages.

_____ Like

Comment:

2012
In order to get what u need u have to answer this question, who r u connected to?

_____ Like

Comment:

2014
Do your good deeds. You may or may not get a thank you, but you are getting the credit.

_____ Like

Comment:

January 7
2013
Prayer, church, exercise, eating right, good attitude, loving ur neighbor is a lifestyle, not an occasion.

_____ Like

Comment:

2014
5 degrees for winter, what else would you expect?

_____ Like

Comment:

January 8
2013
It's heavy bc you are not strong.

_____ Like

Comment:

2014
You say, "don't throw me under the bus." You are already under the bus as a consistently shady person.

_____ Like

Comment:

January 9
2012
Thanks for favor Lord Jesus.

_____ Like

Comment:

2013
Resilience that's what u got. The ability to bounce back. Walk in it today.

_____ Like

Comment:

2014
Do you ever think you'll run out of ideas to post? Naw, I think not, you are much too wise.

_____ Like

Comment:

2015
Somebody's got to do it, it don't have to be you, but it might as well be you. There's a shelf asking you for your book.

_____ Like

Comment:

January 10
2011
Really take a minute n think about this one, if God is for u, then who can be against u. Romans 8:31. Be blessed!

_____ Like

Comment:

2012
Where I am going is much better than where I've been.

_____ Like

Comment:

2013
U don't sit around waiting for things to happen. U make things happen. That's what I like about u.

_____ Like

Comment:

2014
When I got my first car, my cousin Edward who sold insurance told me, "cuz you are going to have to pay the cost to be the boss." Those words still ring true. No success without some sacrifice.

Have a great day, it's better than having a good day.

_____ Like

Comment:

January 11
2012
In the movie "Blood Diamond, Djimon Hounsou told hid son who he was n he won his son back. Today I am reminded of whose "I Am" n who I am.

_____ Like

Comment:

2013
There's a solution to your problem. Slow down and ask for God's free wisdom.

_____ Like

Comment:

2015
The day will come when their comments won't affect you the same because you'll be stronger.

_____ Like

Comment:

January 12
2012
Some people will never forget ur past, shame on them. "if the Son sets u free, u will be free indeed." John 8:36

_____ Like

Comment:

January 13
2012
Some say, "n u supposed to be a Christian." U r, but they might not know grade u r in. Next time tell them u r a _____ grader Christian. We r not all n the same grade.

_____ Like

Comment:

2014
People are always important, but their stuff might not be.

_____ Like

Comment:

January 14
2013
Life does move on, but do you?

_____ Like

Comment:

2014
You study, you pray and you believe now it's time for God to do the rest.

_____ Like

Comment:

January 15
2013
U believe, but where is ur action. bc faith without works is dead. James 2:17

_____ Like

Comment:

2014
God gives us the power to achieve. We give ourselves the permission.

_____ Like

Comment:

My son told me, "when I get older dad I'm going to fix food for you."I can't wait.

_____ Like

Comment:

January 16
2012
What a prophet, Martin Luther King Jr. May we all strive to fulfill ur dream of being EXCELLENT

_____ Like

Comment:

2013
U may be tired n sleepy, but never lose ur willingness.

_____ Like

Comment:

January 17
2012
I'm determined. I'm not lazy

Would someone tell my son that McDonalds don't cook French fries this early.

_____ Like

Comment:

2013
You are an atmospheric changer when u show up.

_____ Like

Comment:

2014
You are stronger than you think. Don't get it twisted.

_____ Like

Comment:

January 18
2011
The God I serve is amazing, u don't know, u better ask somebody!

_____ Like

Comment:

2013

I am gonna live a healthy holistic life.

_____ Like

Comment:

January 19

2011

Have u stopped to think about just how good a life u have, in spite of.

I dare u to go God behind my back n talk about me.

_____ Like

Comment:

2012

I'm so glad I'm not who I use to be. Make me more like u Lord Jesus

_____ Like

Comment:

2015

You don't want to miss Dr. Cindy Trimm, if you are serious about going to another level.

_____ Like

Comment:

January 20
2012
If my son can request the yellow juice at 6 am (orange juice), than the blue potty request must be soon.

_____ Like

Comment:

2014
Just post to be posting. U never know who you will make laugh or inspire.

_____ Like

Comment:

January 21
2013
These kids are having so much fun at Chick Fila.

_____ Like

Comment:

2014
There's more to you than what we see, at the right time we are all going to see your magnificence.

_____ Like

Comment:

January 22
2013

Wherever u are. Whatever u might be doing. U can give The Lord praise.

_____ Like

Comment:

I've been put out the bathroom by my son, "I need my privacy" is what he tells me. He doesn't know how happy I am.

_____ Like

Comment:

Crab dip all the way. — at Koco's Pub.

_____ Like

Comment:

2014

Aren't you glad God is always there?

_____ Like

Comment:

January 23
2012

U say, "I'll just be five minutes late." Why not say, "I'll just be five minutes early."Change ur mindset n u will change ur future.

_____ Like

Comment:

2013

You can't sit still u got to move.

_____ Like

Comment:

2014

The question is not can you do it, but will you do it?

_____ Like

Comment:

January 24
2011

I have been paying dearly for procrastinating, please don't procrastinate. Now is the time.

_____ Like

Comment:

2012

N those times when u don't know what u should say, it's ok to be silent.

_____ Like

Comment:

"Even a fool is thought wise if he keeps silent, and discerning if he holds his tongue." Proverbs 17:28

2013

Count the cost. Is it really worth fighting for?

2014

If you love someone, it should not be in word only, but sometimes in deed.

_____ Like

Comment:

2015

He is 'bout to roll at his first soccer game.

_____ Like

Comment:

January 25
2012

I'm gonna throw myself a party n dance, dance, dance.

_____ Like

Comment:

2013

There's a zero percent chance u can change ur past, but a 100 percent chance u can change ur future.

_____ Like

Comment:

January 26
2012

Did u know that the 2nd most common illicit (unlawful) drug is Cocaine (powdered n Crack) in the USA?

n studies, rats have chosen Cocaine over food, sex and water. N would die for it. People behave similarly.

Jesus can deliver u from Cocaine addiction, if u would believe. It's called spontane-
ous recovery in the addiction world. "because nothing shall be impossible with God."
Luke 1:37

_____ Like

Comment:

January 27
2014

If you don't do it, who else will?

_____ Like

Comment:

January 28
2011

I'm actually liking Sponge Bob Squarepants and I think Dora the Explorer is cool.

_____ Like

Comment:

2013

U do little, but ask for a lot. Shame on you.

_____ Like

Comment:

Usually I post in the am, but ive been thinking bout u. U think nobodys watching u, but they r. There is excellence in you and it's about to come forth. One more thing, You are so exemplary.

_____ Like

Comment:

2014

This Saturday I will be showcasing "Mixing." The public is invited, while this is not a book signing, it is a opportunity to sharpen my skills. Check it out:Black Writers Guild Member Showcase on Saturday, February 1st at 1 p.m. (Enoch Pratt Library, Pennsylvania Avenue Branch, 1531 W. North Avenue, Baltimore).

_____ Like

Comment:

It's exciting you have a business, but you have to be busy and organized.

_____ Like

Comment:

I was thinking what if you could remember everything you read especially the Word of God. You would be a powerhouse.

_____ Like

Comment:

January 29
2015
You are not the only one who can do that, but you are the only one who can do it that way. "Unique", that's who you are.

_____ Like

Comment:

January 30
2012
U say, "but they don't like me." They don't have to. But u need to like u

_____ Like

Comment:

2013
When u put things back in the same place. U have peace when u look for it later.

_____ Like

Comment:

2014
Favor is before you and motivation is behind you.

_____ Like

Comment:

January 31
2011
I won't look back.

_____ Like

Comment:

2012
Just taking notice of all this technology, I think it is given so that we may have "an abundant life.""I am come that they might have life, and that they might have it more abundantly." John 10:10 b

_____ Like

Comment:

2013
You have the time to do what u want, u just need to find the will.

_____ Like

Comment:

My son says, he has been putting money in his tv, "so it can work." I laughed at first bc I had a nephew who did the same thing as a kid. I am curious about what he will put in the tv when it breaks.

_____ Like

Comment:

2014

A component to a good day is a good nights sleep. Get one.

_____ Like

Comment:

CHAPTER 2
February

February 1
2013

Jesus.

_____ Like

Comment:

February 2
2012

There's was a time I would "go off" about a situation, now I don't react with a comment. I'm changing. I like it.

_____ Like

Comment:

February 3
2012

Not gonna talk about it. Gonna do something about it.

_____ Like

Comment:

Just learned that a 2 year old flosses. Never to old to learn something new.

_____ Like

Comment:

2014

What would I be without you Lord? I be lost.

_____ Like

Comment:

February 4
2013

When u want it bad enough, u will make an all-out effort. "Blessed are those who hunger and thirst for righteousness, for they will be filled." Matthew 5:6

_____ Like

Comment:

2014

I think time management is more important than money management bc "time is money."

_____ Like

Comment:

February 5
2011

Tasha Cobbs says "where would I be without you." Where would u be?

_____ Like

Comment:

2013

I almost gave up. Looking for my cap this morning, couldn't seem to find it.
I went to the place were I always place it, but couldn't seem to find it, then I
thought I'll have to wear a hat. Then I looked one more time n it was there, just
had to not give up.

_____ Like

Comment:

2014

You are not a mess, but a message. Define yourself and you'll be less to accept the
definition of who you are from others.

_____ Like

Comment:

February 6
2012

Josephine Jordan, my mom and one of the wisest woman I know bout to make it n
the Black History books.

_____ Like

Comment:

2013

Where would I be without you Lord? I'd be lost.

_____ Like

Comment:

2014

There's a book n you, so when do we get to read it.

_____ Like

Comment:

February 7

2011

"The King's Speech" superb movie. You got to go see it before the Oscars.

_____ Like

Comment:

2012

Get a habit for doing what is right.

_____ Like

Comment:

2013

Know that it is your faith that moves God.

_____ Like

Comment:

2014

I had all these thoughts but no time to put them in written form. Now I can tell you what I'm thinking, enjoy this n everyday. Let no one be responsible for your happiness.

_____ Like

Comment:

February 8
2012
Just bc u spoke it doesn't mean I heard u or understand u. If u want to be certain just ask me.

_____ Like

Comment:

2013
The devil says, "Jesus I know and I know you too."

_____ Like

Comment:

February 9
2011
use to wake up thinkin bout what I coulda or shouldav done. now I think bout what I'm gonna do. don't let your past rob u of your future.

_____ Like

Comment:

2012
Learning to delay instant pleasure for long term peace.

_____ Like

Comment:

2014
If I don't believe in me, why should you?

_____ Like

Comment:

February 10
2012
I'm excited! Can u get excited with me even if u don't have the details.

_____ Like

Comment:

2013
This morning Goshen asked for a bowl, spoon and grape juice. He asked if I would pour the juice into the bowl, then he began to drink it one spoon at a time. It's good to think out the box.

_____ Like

Comment:

2015
Church is a place for you to grow spiritually.

_____ Like

Comment:

February 11
2011
thank you Lord. in all things give him thanks 1 Thess. 5:18

_____ Like

Comment:

2013
Your faith will be tested, but remember ur help comes from The Lord.

_____ Like

Comment:

2014

Information given doesn't equal information received. You have to buy into or believe the information.

_____ Like

Comment:

2015

If you wait til tomorrow to do what you can do today, don't get mad at me if I do it today.

_____ Like

Comment:

February 12

2013

It is said, one phone call or contact can change the course of your destiny for the good. Yesterday, I believe I received that call,

_____ Like

Comment:

2015

Part of who you are is because of your exposures in life, change your exposures and you will change your life.

_____ Like

Comment:

2016

You and I don't have perfect lives, but we have purposeful lives.

_____ Like

Comment:

February 13

2012

Lord Jesus show me off for your glory. In the same way, let your light shine before others, that they may see your good deeds and glorify your Father in heaven. (Matthew 5:16 NIV)

_____ Like

Comment:

2013

Valentine's Day is tomorrow, but God loves us with an everlasting love. Show ur love to ur neighbor.

_____ Like

Comment:

2014

There's no question that this is winter.

_____ Like

Comment:

February 14
2011
How can I forget Him?

_____ Like

Comment:

2012
What's simple for u, maybe complicated to me. Don't judge me.

_____ Like

Comment:

2013
Stop trying to get some people to fly with you. They can't handle the altitude.

_____ Like

Comment:

2013
I think one of the greatest joys is to hear someone say, "I love you" and you know that they mean it.

_____ Like

Comment:

February 15
2012
"What u see is what u get" - Flip Wilson aka Geraldine. No more hiding.

_____ Like

Comment:

February 16
2012
Be humble n u will be exalted. Matthew 7. Understood the exalting. Had to learn the humbling.

_____ Like

Comment:

2016
Goshen wrote me a note tonight.

_____ Like

Comment:

February 17
2012
Replace ur "what ifs" and "but" with "I can n I will" Stop wasting time.

_____ Like

Comment:

2014
Trust in the Lord. Rely, depend, have confidence, strongly believe and don't doubt.

_____ Like

Comment:

2016
You don't need a title or position, to do people right.

_____ Like

Comment:

February 18
2013
There's so much n life to do, why waste your time. Being productive, purposeful and positive today.

_____ Like

Comment:

2014
You did it, you got there, you made it, just in the nick of time.

_____ Like

Comment:

2016
If you are going to write a book, you must spend at least 10 minutes a day, 5 - 7 days of the week. This is what a wise man told me at the Baltimore Book Festival in 2006, it works.

_____ Like

Comment:

February 19
2013
will say like my good brother Apostle Paul, "when I am weak, then I am strong."2 Corinthians 12:10Paul had one conversion and never turned back.

_____ Like

Comment:

2014

You got that title because that's what you do, not who you are. You are so much bigger.

_____ Like

Comment:

2015

One day I'll speak and most of the people in Baltimore will hear me www.mccraylectures.com

_____ Like

Comment:

2016

I have to remind myself that rejection is a prerequisite for success.

_____ Like

Comment:

Hanging out with sister Lucy and brother Lewis, movie night!

_____ Like

Comment:

February 20
2012

I told u when UPS delivers I would shout n dance. Well I'm just rejoicing n my heart. The world is about to know about a special woman. Momma may heaven allow u to peek at what I'm holding n my hands.

_____ Like

Comment:

2013

Welcome back Robin from Good Morning America! You are so sweet.

_____ Like

Comment:

2014

Listen to your body, it speaks.

_____ Like

Comment:

February 21

2012

U know this is a special day when ur toddler says, "give me a kiss, see u later."

_____ Like

Comment:

2013

Don't be selfish. Your gifts and talents are not just for you. Bless us all!

_____ Like

Comment:

2014

What value do place on you or do you wait to be valued by others?

_____ Like

Comment:

2015

I give Goshen a dollar for a drink, that cost .50 cents, he comes back needing more money. I say, "why?" Turns out, he is buying a little girl something to drink too. smh.

_____ Like

Comment:

February 22
2012

I'm not too busy that I can't stop to say, thank you Jesus.

_____ Like

Comment:

2013

Please stop talking about folks, instead let them talk about what a blessing you are, how you are so loving, how you are so giving. Let them talk about u and great will be your reward.

_____ Like

Comment:

February 23
2012

Testimony: had a slow bathroom drain all week. Plumber called n was scheduled to arrive this am. In the middle of the night drain opened n no plumber needed, thank you Jesus.

_____ Like

Comment:

2015

Baltimore offers online training for heroin antidote. baltimoresun.com
We're trying to make a difference.
Your brain was fine, until you added drugs and alcohol to it.
_____ Like
Comment:

February 24
2012

God sets the lonely in families, Psalm 68:6 A (New International Version)U should never be alone.
_____ Like
Comment:

The founder of FB gave us the power to release our words n now he is a billionaire. How much could u get if u apply ur words?
_____ Like
Comment:

2014

You sit there worried about what are they going to say, when God has already told you what to do. I can't believe you. You believe in man more than you believe in God.
_____ Like
Comment:

February 25
2013
The joy to living this life, is knowing that you are going somewhere and you are enjoying the ride.

_____ Like

Comment:

2014
It's not hard to come up with words to say, but the right ones require some careful thought. Be mindful.

_____ Like

Comment:

February 26
2013
Aren't you glad that u have a habit to pray.

_____ Like

Comment:

2014
The sacrifice now is so you can enjoy the later.

_____ Like

Comment:

2016

This morning I asked Goshen was he going to get a goal in soccer. He said, "no, my teammates won't let me."I said, "go after the ball and get a goal."Today, he scored two goals and their first team win. We are so excited and proud of him!

_____ Like

Comment:

February 27
2012

I'm excited, no more waiting. Sometimes we wait for the right moment. This is it!

_____ Like

Comment:

"Safe House" action packed. Great spy movie. Denzel is da man.

_____ Like

Comment:

2013

Forgiveness, we all need it.

_____ Like

Comment:

2014

The Apostle Paul said in Romans 1 that he served God with his whole heart, that's what I'll do too.

_____ Like

Comment:

The seatbelt is not just for you, but the people that love you too.

_____ Like

Comment:

2015

I believe I can fly (achieve, succeed and overcome).

_____ Like

Comment:

2016

Hanging out with the soccer champ.

_____ Like

Comment:

February 28
2012

Ur enemies r no match for ur God.

_____ Like

Comment:

2013

Talk less about it, but do more about it.

_____ Like

Comment:

2014

Never too busy to be kind, good morning to you all.

_____ Like

Comment:

February 29
2012

Don't forget the people who held you up when u were weak.

_____ Like

Comment:

CHAPTER 3
March

March 1
2012

Aren't u glad u know Wisdom n when she calls out u respond. Does not wisdom call out? Proverbs 8:1

_____ Like

Comment:

Even though the cuff links were found with the Mattel cars, I'm still happy I found them.

_____ Like

Comment:

2013

Whatever u do today, don't be afraid.

_____ Like

Comment:

March 2
2012
Affirmations n confirmations r good but determination is better.

_____ Like

Comment:

2014
Had a fun time demonstrating the power of mixing. Shared with the guest how to get started with writing a book and promoting your book. Signed many copies of "Mixing" and met a lot of new people. Don't wait for a signing to get your copy. "Mixing" is available on Amazon.com. Thanks Lucy for sharing your home and being a shining light (meaning of Lucy).

_____ Like

Comment:

March 3
2014
I've been invited to a snow fight with a preschooler. I can't wait.

_____ Like

Comment:

March 4
2013
I'm honest today. Not afraid of what people think about me. Again, I'm honest today.

_____ Like

Comment:

2014

New order: read the Word of God, review finances, then post on FB.

_____ Like

Comment:

March 5

2012

I'm "pushing on" n I'm strong. If you fail under pressure, your strength is too small.
Proverbs 20:14New Living Translation (©2007)

_____ Like

Comment:

2013

Bc I've prepared for this day, my response to you will be different.

_____ Like

Comment:

2014

I was thinking and maybe you have thought this, why am I doing this? It's because your steps are ordered by The Lord.

_____ Like

Comment:

March 6

2012

I like a person who is "pushing on" in spite of their circumstances.

_____ Like

Comment:

2013

I do believe if u would forget about the things behind and reach into ur future. U would go to a higher place in God. That's what Paul did, see Philippians 3:13-14

_____ Like

Comment:

2014

My better is coming, be on the lookout for yours.

_____ Like

Comment:

2016

First the bike, next the car.

_____ Like

Comment:

March 7
2012

People r talking about u. U just don't know what they r saying. It could be positive or negative, but u can't stop them. Live ur life.

_____ Like

Comment:

Oh by the way, did I tell u my book, "Pushing On" is on Amazon.com selling. Also, I have invited many to the book signing this month too. Get ur book today it will bless u!

_____ Like

Comment:

As I was coming home I heard this song. "I see increase all around me. Stretch forth enlarge my territory." Israel Houghton.

_____ Like

Comment:

2013

Decided not to refinance. Got to have the peace with every major decision. No "aha" or peace, don't do it.

_____ Like

Comment:

2014

I asked Goshen if he knew that I wrote a book and he said, "yes." I asked him if he knew the name of it and he said, "Mixing," then he said, "what is mixing?" I told him it was about kissing and he said, "I'm not going to kiss anybody anymore, maybe one kiss." Lol If a four year old knows about "Mixing," so should you.

_____ Like

Comment:

I'm stronger now. I use to cry and complain. Now I stand tall and face my foes knowing that if God be for me, who can be against me?

_____ Like

Comment:

2015

When you are confident in who you are, but not cocky, you will be a force to be reckoned with and your fruit will remain.

_____ Like

Comment:

March 8
2013

May I live the life I post about.

_____ Like

Comment:

2017

Become a voracious reader and a fearless leader.

_____ Like

Comment:

March 9

2012

Just one word can change the course of ur life, if u believe that word.

_____ Like

Comment:

2015

Don't let one bad instance spoil your whole day, you can regroup.

_____ Like

Comment:

2016

If you could get a look inside your body and see all the awesome work it is doing, you would take better care of yourself. I believe that.

_____ Like

Comment:

March 10
2014
Some never before exciting things are happening for me. Would you be happy for me because the wait is over?

_____ Like

Comment:

2015
No distractions will keep you from the prize because your eyes are fixed on it.

_____ Like

Comment:

2016
You ever worry about something and found out later it wasn't that heavy? Your load is lighter than it appears.

_____ Like

Comment:

2017
I will never claim to know everything, but this one I know, "as the Father has loved me, so have I loved you. Now remain in my love." John 15:9

_____ Like

Comment:

March 11
2013
You are expected to just show up and the rest is history.
_____ Like
Comment:

2014
Don't pray that storms not come, but instead pray for an umbrella in the storm.
_____ Like
Comment:

2015
My son brings me food from the restaurant yesterday and he says, "orders up," then he sits there and begins to help himself to my food.
When does the waiter or cook help themselves to the customers' food?
_____ Like
Comment:

2016
When Jesus ask you to follow him, you are going places.
_____ Like
Comment:

March 12
2012
If u sit n wait, that's on u. If u miss an opportunity, that's on u. U see, how it's up to u.

_____ Like

Comment:

2013
Remember,"you walk by faith, not by sight." 2 Corin. 5:7Don't be caught up in how it appears now, it is subject to change.

_____ Like

Comment:

2014
A singer sings. A waiter serves. A cook cooks. A giver gives. A writer writes. So, what are you waiting for, do who you are.

_____ Like

Comment:

I thought today about bills n fees, then I thought about provision n blessings. The two are inseparable.

_____ Like

Comment:

March 13

2011

look in the mirror n say to yourself "I am _____." Now smile.

_____ Like

Comment:

2012

If u r not excited about ur product or service, why should I be?

_____ Like

Comment:

2013

You say words are not powerful. Let's see, you are wise, giving, loving, kind, full of wisdom, purposeful, fearfully and wonderfully made, on time, destined for greatness and humble.

_____ Like

Comment:

2014

Respect - To take notice of; to regard with special attention; to regard as worthy of special consideration; hence, to care for; to heed.

Respect yourself.

_____ Like

Comment:

2015

Get into the habit of praying. You are more powerful than you think.

_____ Like

Comment:

2016

Make a habit to eat at least one nutritious meal a day.

_____ Like

Comment:

March 14
2012

U r holding ur head up because "u r looking to the hills which comes ur help, n ur help comes from the Lord" Psalms 121:1

_____ Like

Comment:

2013

Only necessary words. "Those who guard their lips preserve their lives, but those who speak rashly will come to ruin." Proverbs 13:3

_____ Like

Comment:

2014

It's gonna be a great day because you are a part of it.

_____ Like

Comment:

2016

We pick what's important to us. One day, what was important, may not be important anymore. May you always know the power of your will?

_____ Like

Comment:

March 15
2013

"Appreciation Day" Today, go out of your way to let someone know how much you appreciate them.

_____ Like

Comment:

March 16
2012

When u begin to see yourself like God sees u, u will never see ur self the same again. Thank u Lord for changing my self-image.

_____ Like

Comment:

2015

If you want to be doing some big things in the kingdom, you should come worship at Dreamlife Worship Center under the leadership of Pastor Kenneth O. Robinson Jr. I'm willing to fulfill my dreams, what about you?

_____ Like

Comment:

2017

You can have the greater, but it comes with persecution. Do you still want it?1 Peter 4:12-14

_____ Like

Comment:

March 17
2014

I looked outside and Winter said, "what are you looking at, I'm just doing my thing."

_____ Like

Comment:

March 18
2013

You may suffer awhile, but God... 1 Peter 5:10

_____ Like

Comment:

2014

What are the odds that you will succeed, very high, if you believe?

_____ Like

Comment:

2015

You're not going to like everybody and everybody is not going to like you, accept it and move on, you have bigger fish to fry. The above has been said before, but sometimes we need a reminder.

_____ Like

Comment:

March 19
2013

It takes great courage to do what u do. Keep doing great things.

_____ Like

Comment:

2014

I woke up with good things on my mind.

_____ Like

Comment:

2015

The key to listening is to be quiet.

_____ Like

Comment:

March 20
2012

Look for the lesson in the situation. If u learn the lesson u won't be too upset about the situation.

_____ Like

Comment:

2013

Sometimes we don't appreciate our body til it doesn't work as well. Take good care of your body.

_____ Like

Comment:

2014

I am learning to wait for the better.

_____ Like

Comment:

March 21
2012

Don't waste time on people or things that don't move u forward.

_____ Like

Comment:

2013

Why are you looking for great results, when you put in mere effort. Don't fool yourself. U reap what u sow. Gal. 6:7

_____ Like

Comment:

2014

You can literally change your atmosphere, just by praising God. There will be atmospheric changes today in my life.

_____ Like

Comment:

March 22
2013

Family time is precious. Yesterday sat around the fire with wife and son and enjoyed their presence.

_____ Like

Comment:

2014

amazon.com

"Mixing" is my new eye opening, informative, funny and inspiring book. I put a spin on the topic of sex in this book as I challenge the reader to look at the preciousness of sex. Mixing means sexual intimacy and is a book born out of a desire to see people have a greater appreciation of their bodies as it comes to mixing.

_____ Like

Comment:

2017

Stick to your routine, it's working for you.

_____ Like

Comment:

March 23
2012

U say, "why should I take medicine for high blood pressure, when I feel ok." I say when u start to not feel right. It might be too late. The damage is done. Comply now, so u can live long n strong.

_____ Like

Comment:

2015

Your opposition is based on your assignment.

_____ Like

Comment:

March 24
2014

You feel resistance bc you are moving forward.

_____ Like

Comment:

2017

- When you are passionate about something, you will pursue it to the end. President Obama was passionate about health care reform.
  _____ Like
Comment:

- Your haters are secretly your motivators.
  _____ Like
Comment:

March 25
2013

Don't let nothing get in your way of doing the will of your God.
_____ Like
Comment:

2014

I pray for the God of peace to go before you today.

2015

Sometimes Jesus will let you see a person's true colors, so you can get your eyes back on him. Looking unto Jesus the author and finisher of our faith; Hebrews 12:2
_____ Like
Comment:

March 26

2013

If u can't afford it now, then wait. You'll get a better opportunity later.

_____ Like

Comment:

2014

It takes much effort to balance this body, mind and spirit.

_____ Like

Comment:

March 27

2013

After all I done, thank you Jesus for dying for me and rising the third day.

_____ Like

Comment:

2014

You can post about God, then live like God.

_____ Like

Comment:

2015

The love of God is amazing.

_____ Like

Comment:

March 28
2013
Once u get a few more enemies, then God can prepare the table. He prepares a table in the presence of my enemies (plural). Psalms 23
_____ Like
Comment:

2014
I want to read and learn the more.
_____ Like
Comment:

March 29
2013
You have to have a "I can do it attitude" in these times.
_____ Like
Comment:

2014
www.eduftc.com
Started Education For The Community, LLC December 2011 to educate the community about drug addiction, HIV/AIDS and mental illness. A lot of pro bono lectures, but today check was in the mail!U shall repeat, if u faint not. Galatians 6:9
_____ Like
Comment:

2017

The adversity can make you stronger, but you are strong before the adversity.

_____ Like

Comment:

March 30
2017

I desire to be more spiritually minded and less carnally minded.

_____ Like

Comment:

March 31
2014

The thING will come to pass, not just wishING, prayING or sayING, but doING.

_____ Like

Comment:

2017

Don't unfriend another one of your enemies, that's not kind to treat your dinner guest that way. "You prepare a table before me in the presence of my enemies." Psalm 23:5a

_____ Like

Comment:

CHAPTER 4
April

April 1
2013
Fiber One for breakfast, naturally lowering cholesterol. This is my body. Who said I can't improve it.

_____ Like

Comment:

2014
You ever woke up with so much to do? Before u get going with ur busy day, give thanks.

_____ Like

Comment:

April 2
2012
Got to get up early n prepare for a victorious day.

_____ Like

Comment:

2013

Just in case u get busy n forget, the Lord is good.

_____ Like

Comment:

2014

If you spend your time focused on people n their drama, you will not be focused on yourself n your drama.

_____ Like

Comment:

April 3

2011

u can't grow if ur not planted.

_____ Like

Comment:

2012

I'm gonna get it done n u r not gonna waste my time.

_____ Like

Comment:

2013

There are infants, toddlers, preschoolers, elementary school, middle school, high school and college mature Christian. Be careful when u judge one of them. They just might be performing at their correct level.

_____ Like

Comment:

2014

It's easier to see what's in front of you, than what's behind you. Keeping looking forward.

_____ Like

Comment:

2017

- You might want it, but how bad do you want it and what sacrifices are you willing to make to have it?

_____ Like

Comment:

- I've been invited to attend class with my son. These kids are interesting. Pray for our teachers.

_____ Like

Comment:

April 4

2012

Today I invite criticism, so that I might taste success.

_____ Like

Comment:

2013

It gets better. You'll see.

_____ Like

Comment:

2014

You can:Prey on me with your mouth or pray for me with your mouth. I hope you choose the latter.

_____ Like

Comment:

2016

If you are going to succeed, you got to hustle. You can have it, when you can afford it, it's just that simple.

_____ Like

Comment:

2017

Has Facebook replaced our personal diaries? smh

_____ Like

Comment:

April 5
2016

- You can read a verse, a paragraph or a chapter of the Word of God and be blessed. The Word is rich, take advantage of it.

_____ Like

Comment:

- Up and on the move, no time to waste.

_____ Like

Comment:

2017

Don't let a "no" stop your pursuit of a "yes."

_____ Like

Comment:

April 6
2012

U say but Lord I have desires and the reply is "Psalm 37:3-4New King James Version (NKJV)3 Trust in the Lord, and do good;Dwell in the land, and feed on His faithfulness.4 Delight yourself also in the Lord, And He shall give you the desires of your heart."I believe that.

_____ Like

Comment:

2015

Sometimes we can't have new success, because we are holding on to old failures.

_____ Like

Comment:

2016

I'm a soldier in the army of the Lord.

_____ Like

Comment:

2017

Don't fall into the trap of thinking your past failures are still with you. This is a new day, rejoice!

_____ Like

Comment:

April 7
2014

Some might say you are bragging.

I say you are just confident. You know what you want out of life and it shows.

_____ Like

Comment:

2015

Time is a good friend of mine.

_____ Like

Comment:

April 8
2013
To err is human, but to lie is a choice.

_____ Like

Comment:

2014
When u realize ur potential, u will never again waste time or money.

_____ Like

Comment:

April 9
2012
Moving forward n pushing on. We are troubled on every side, yet not distressed; we are perplexed, but not in despair; Persecuted, but not forsaken; cast down, but not destroyed; (2 Corinthians 4:8, 9 KJV)

_____ Like

Comment:

2013
Be determined today to complete it regardless of how u feel or what others may think of u.

_____ Like

Comment:

2014

You are just getting started.

_____ Like

Comment:

2016

It's two slices of wheat toast with jelly, it's better for me than a Cinnamelt at McDonald's -cheaper and more nutritional.

_____ Like

Comment:

April 10

2012

U say, "I'll get it done,"but when?Ecclesiastes 5:3New King James Version (NKJV)3 For a dream comes through much activity, And a fool's voice is known by his many words.

_____ Like

Comment:

2013

Addiction is cunning, baffling and powerful, but treatable. www.mccraylectures.com

_____ Like

Comment:

2014

You can't change my mind. My greater is coming.

_____ Like

Comment:

2015

Pray.

_____ Like

Comment:

2017

When you make a promise to kids they don't forget it and neither do grown ups.

_____ Like

Comment:

April 11
2012

R u mostly a contributor or a taker?Give, u shall receive. Take, n u will repay.

_____ Like

Comment:

2013

I think two very powerful words are "thank you." So, let me say, thank you for accepting my friend request, letting me know sometimes you like what I post, praying for me, feeding me, visiting me, calling me, inspiring me with your post, inviting me to your affairs, keeping in contact with me after all these years, wishing me well, buying my book and reading it too, hoping the best for me, enjoying the pictures of my son, wishing my family well. Lastly, I do hope that you know I appreciate and thank you.

_____ Like

Comment:

2014

One of the greatest mysteries revealed is how God would choose to abide or live in me through Jesus.

_____ Like

Comment:

2016

Just a talk with Jesus, gives me a new perspective on the situation.

_____ Like

Comment:

April 12
2013

You like trash worthy talk, but you should have wholesome worthy talk coming out of your mouth. Be careful talking trash will prepare u to be a trashcan. Further help is found in Ephesians 4:29

_____ Like

Comment:

2016

Shawanda Clark-McCray you are beautiful.

_____ Like

Comment:

April 13
2012

I am purposeful today.

_____ Like

Comment:

2017

Aren't you glad you're not a quitter?

_____ Like

Comment:

April 14
2014

I'm not thinking just about myself, but I want you to succeed and be happy too.

_____ Like

Comment:

2017

It's good to be the younger sibling and have a loving sister named "Lucille," who treats you to the movie.

_____ Like

Comment:

April 15
2013

Great weekend with my families (nuclear, immediate and church). Fellowship is powerful don't forsake it.

_____ Like

Comment:

2016

I believe things are going to change for you. Do you believe it too?

_____ Like

Comment:

April 16
2012

Kenny u went far above what I paid for to give me twice as many pics. The pictures are superb. May your business grow the more n Jesus Name. I'm so excited.

_____ Like

Comment:

2013

This is not optional, it is not based on a like or comment, but we must always pray n not cease.

_____ Like

Comment:

2014

Breakfast with Goshen, what a way to start my day, thanks son.

_____ Like

Comment:

April 17
2012

U need n idea n some motivation.

_____ Like

Comment:

2013

You're going to do this n you're going to do that, but what are you really doing?

_____ Like

Comment:

2014

I believe no one can stop you from fulfilling your dream when you are driven by passion.

_____ Like

Comment:

2016

Family is fun. — at Regal Cinemas Hunt Valley 12.

_____ Like

Comment:

2017

- You can wait for things to happen or you can make things happen.

  _____ Like

Comment:

- When you are too busy to pray, read God's Word, minister to people in need or show love; I agree with you. You are too busy.

  _____ Like

Comment:

April 18
2013

My laters have become my nows.

_____ Like

Comment:

2014

As a former high school runner, I remember hard work earned me victory, the same is true today. Do you not know that in a race all the runners run, but only one gets the prize? Run in such a way as to get the prize. 1 Corinthians 9:24

_____ Like

Comment:

2017

They are "naysayers" because they always say "no.""No, you can't do that. No, that won't work. No, you shouldn't try that. Change who you hang out with and you'll change your future.

_____ Like

Comment:

April 19
2012

Have a powerful day.

_____ Like

Comment:

2013

- Pursue your passion and get ultimate fulfillment.

_____ Like

Comment:

- We anxiously spend the money but patiently pay it back. I think it should be the opposite.

_____ Like

Comment:

2016

- You can know better. but not do better. Knowledge is good, but doing what you know is better.

  _____ Like

Comment:

- For all your facing, I'm amazed at how well you look.

  _____ Like

Comment:

April 20
2012

- If u don't ask, don't get mad when u don't have. James 4:3 said it first

  _____ Like

Comment:

- U say, "but I want to be successful"What problem will u solve or question will u answer - Dan Poynter

  _____ Like

Comment:

2017

Our good, will get better and our better will get greater. You just watch and see!

_____ Like

Comment:

April 21
2011
bout to eat at Cracker Barrel, so tell me why is our son eating his shoe.

_____ Like

Comment:

2014
You say, "I would do it, but I'm afraid."Hold on to courage and do it anyway.

_____ Like

Comment:

2017
We want to accomplish "item B," but "item A" remains outstanding. One step at a time is how it's done.

_____ Like

Comment:

April 22
2013
- I might look the same, but I sure don't think the same.

_____ Like

Comment:

- You are not anointed to gossip. An anointing is a special gift for a special task. Anyone can gossip.

_____ Like

Comment:

2014

Don't let people pimp ur negative side, instead show them the good in you.

_____ Like

Comment:

April 23

2011

- God loves me and there is nothing I can do about it.

_____ Like

Comment:

- Its amazing all the stuff aka junk n the garage. what am I saving it for?

_____ Like

Comment:

2012

Checked out "Think Like a Man" with my big brother Lewis. Great, funny and thought provoking movie. A must see!

_____ Like

Comment:

2013

Sometimes we miss it, but don't brutalize yourself, just try it again. Been there done that, it hurts.

_____ Like

Comment:

2014

Whatever time or place isn't as important as making time to pray.

_____ Like

Comment:

April 24
2013

I don't see what you see. I see greatness.

_____ Like

Comment:

2014

It's not that much about talk as it is about your walk. May the two catch up with each other.

_____ Like

Comment:

April 25
2013

Sometimes I post by faith, not by sight.

_____ Like

Comment:

2014

I see it as a passion and a purpose, not a position and a paycheck.

_____ Like

Comment:

2016

Yesterday, Goshen told me, "dad you have to eat vegetables, so you can live to 100."I told him how old he would be and that I will. His insight amazes me.

_____ Like

Comment:

2017

- May you stay focus today and ignore the distractions because you and I are going to some big places.

_____ Like

Comment:

- What you say is liked, more than people will admit.

_____ Like

Comment:

April 26

2012

Before u give up, Make sure u have done all. After Having done all, to standEphesians 6:13

_____ Like

Comment:

2013

We pray and read God's Word when it's convenient, but we want God in our times of inconvenience.

_____ Like

Comment:

2014

Today was a new frontier. Talking about "Mixing" at the Nile Style Barber Shop. No more fears. But what excited me the most today was when the owner knock off $100 to his barber's weekly rent for those who purchased a book. You should have seen the look on their faces. Nile went to a whole new level for me. What a generous owner and businessman. — with Cassius Williams.

_____ Like

Comment:

April 27

2011

I think whoever learns how to decipher baby talk will make a lot of money.

_____ Like

Comment:

2012

It's all a choice. The food u will eat. The clothes u will wear. The relationship u will have etc. etc. Don't forget the power of your choice.

_____ Like

Comment:

2015

Yesterday I gave my first college lecture to the nursing students at the Baltimore City Community College, my alma mater. We discussed taking care of the drug addicted and alcoholic patient. I had an awesome time and received rave reviews. I can add Adjunct Professor to my resume now. Pursue your dreams good people,

_____ Like

Comment:

April 28
2014

Have you've given thought to who would do it, if you didn't.

_____ Like

Comment:

2015

1 John 5:14 This is the confidence we have in approaching God: that if we ask any-thing according to his will, he hears us. What a promise!

_____ Like

Comment:

2017

The sky is the limit, if you believe what you say.

_____ Like

Comment:

April 29
2013
That which is important will be my focus.

_____ Like

Comment:

2014
New phone, so I missed posting this morning. I rather post in the morning. I wake up with prayer, purpose, passion, potential, power and posts.

_____ Like

Comment:

2016
- I'm wrestling with a project to complete and I can't believe how patient I am. I'm growing.

  _____ Like

Comment:

- It's a beautiful thing to be able to come home to a warm and quiet home. Good night!

  _____ Like

Comment:

April 30
2011
I believe n angels, I just met one today.

_____ Like

Comment:

2012
I asked our son would he use the potty. His reply, "no thanks."Can u believe that.

_____ Like

Comment:

2013
- Always read the signs. The cost of ignoring them can be insurmountable.

_____ Like

Comment:

- The key to being mentally sharp when you are older is being mentally sharp when you were younger.

_____ Like

Comment:

2014
King Solomon prayed for his people, "Teach them the right way to live," 1 Kings 8:36May you be taught the right way to live today.

_____ Like

Comment:

CHAPTER 5

May

May 1
2012
Don't focus on what it looks like bc,"we walk by faith not sight" 2 Corinthians 5:7
_____ Like
Comment:

2013
I can post about Jesus. I can talk about Jesus but more importantly may I live n shine for Jesus.
_____ Like
Comment:

2014
When I think about what I use to do. I know there is a loving God.
_____ Like
Comment:

May 2
2012
If a picture is worth a thousand words, than how much is a motion picture worth?

_____ Like

Comment:

2013
Big sister Lucille McCray-Pinkney taking her Big brother to see "42." I love her so much.

_____ Like

Comment:

2014
One day you are going to do more of what you want to do and less of what you have to do. Stay passionate and purpose driven.

_____ Like

Comment:

May 3
2011
whatever u do today, do it better than u did yesterday.

_____ Like

Comment:

2012
Why do u keep fooling with people who don't support ur vision?
_____ Like
Comment:

2013
The world is waiting for you to change something in it, then you will be called a "World Changer."
_____ Like
Comment:

2016
- You wonder why things are different in your life, retrace your steps of prayer time and reading God's Word and you'll find your answer.
_____ Like
Comment:

- There are some people who keep talking about the old you. They should ask about the new you because you have changed.
_____ Like
Comment:

May 4
2011
today I will be unstoppable n my mission.
_____ Like
Comment:

2012

If u keep thinking about what u want to do is a sign that u should do it. Freedom is the right to do what u want as long as no one else's right r affected.

_____ Like

Comment:

2016

- Tasha Cobb's has been singing in my ear today, "at the end of the day, you still love me."God still loves me, even at the end of the day.

_____ Like

Comment:

- You would never put drugs in you, but you fill up with junk food throughout the day. I'm not saying, I always eat right, but not junk food all day.

_____ Like

Comment:

- Never be satisfied with past successes. Look forward to new ways to be a better you.

_____ Like

Comment:

2017

You prepare like you are going to win and you will.

_____ Like

Comment:

May 5
2014
Happy 13th Anniversary Shawanda Clark-McCray! I love you,
Jose'
_____ Like
Comment:

2017
Happy Wedding Anniversary Shawanda! I love you.
_____ Like
Comment:

May 6
2012
Hi Mrs. Marsha Reeves Jews, I have written wonderful book about my mom and would like to share it with the world on your radio show. The book is called "Pushing On" Wonderful Stories about the Life of Josephine Jordan. Tomorrow I will be on the radio giving my first interview and I am so excited.
_____ Like
Comment:

2013
I love Shawanda because she is my best friend.
_____ Like
Comment:

May 7
2012
Have a make a difference day.

_____ Like

Comment:

2013
You have everything you need to fulfill your purpose. You don't need another reminder.

_____ Like

Comment:

2014
Sometimes when kids do things we don't understand, it can seem strange or bad, but they maybe doing what is normal for their age. Understand their milestones before you judge them.

_____ Like

Comment:

May 8
2011
smile n Happy Mothers Day!

_____ Like

Comment:

2012

U say, "but I'm a good person." well can u be a better than good person.

_____ Like

Comment:

2013

May the people who have come into your life to destroy you, instead elevate you to another level in God.

_____ Like

Comment:

2014

Listen closely to the people talking in your life. See if there conversation lines up with ur dreams, if not lessen the conversation.

_____ Like

Comment:

2017

- Hanging with a cool and intelligent son!

_____ Like

Comment:

- Happy National Nurses Week!Thank you for your excellent service.

_____ Like

Comment:

May 9
2012
Look at you. Full of purpose, power and peace. It's no wonder you attract haters.

_____ Like

Comment:

2013
The easy part is to post it. The hard part is to perform it.

_____ Like

Comment:

2014
Happy Nurses Week! I'm celebrating 28 years of a rewarding and challenging career. Thanks for all the gifts and well wishes.

_____ Like

Comment:

May 10
2012
I don't know about u, but God has been good to me.

_____ Like

Comment:

2013
Last night I just listened to my wife, it was amazing all she had to say. Listening is sometimes more important than being heard.
_____ Like
Comment:

2015
One must balance their checkbook, relationships, time, work and health, just to name a few.
_____ Like
Comment:

2017
Be courageous like a lion and face your jungle.
_____ Like
Comment:

May 11
2011
I have come to realize, I can't waste time.
_____ Like
Comment:

2017

You and I will be stronger after we get through this. "For our present troubles are small and won't last very long. Yet they produce for us a glory that vastly outweighs them and will last forever!" 2 Corinthians 4:17 (New Living Translation)

_____ Like

Comment:

May 12
2011

"just find a need and fill it" taken from the movie Robots.
ever thought about what u would try, if u did not fear failure?

_____ Like

Comment:

2014

Hung out with my wife all day. Cancelled my plans and got some important things done at home. Family is your first ministry.

_____ Like

Comment:

2017

Don't expect to run the race well, if you haven't been practicing.

_____ Like

Comment:

May 13
2013
We want God to hear us and we want hear God, very important.

_____ Like

Comment:

2016
For what you are about to face, your prayer life is about to go to another level.

_____ Like

Comment:

2017
I pray that you will no longer walk in denial about your alcohol and/or drug problem, but that you will seek the help you need, in the name of Jesus.

_____ Like

Comment:

May 14
2012
Today, leave nothing undone. Finish it.

_____ Like

Comment:

2013

A writer is one who is not afraid to share a piece of their mind with the world. Today, I call you all writers.

_____ Like

Comment:

2014

Lust, greed and drugs will allude you. You will feel like you really count, but they do nothing but subtract from your self-worth.

_____ Like

Comment:

2017

We should consider changing it to Happy Mother's Month! You all are so precious, enjoy!

_____ Like

Comment:

May 15

2011

I'm praying for just one more family member to attend the family cookout in June, who didn't attend last year. would you stand in agreement with my prayer.

_____ Like

Comment:

2012

Can u feel the rain? Lord rain down on me.

_____ Like

Comment:

2013

Busy day, late posting. Don't just be busy, but be productive.

_____ Like

Comment:

2014

What is the price of peace? The price varies from person to person.

_____ Like

Comment:

May 16
2011

Have to learn how to accept rejection bc everything n life will not always go my way. Years ago Oprah had a quest on her show that said, "people want to know that they count and belong." I like to echo those words, "u count and u belong."

_____ Like

Comment:

2012

The Body God "I will never leave u or forsake u""In my presence is fullness of joy""If I before u who can be against u"

_____ Like

Comment:

2014

Jesus ask the crippled man in John chapter 5, "do you want to be better or well" (I'm paraphrasing), then he said, "get up, take your mat and walk."I think Jesus coined the term, "just do it," way before Nike.

_____ Like

Comment:

2016

Learn to wait on the request for your advice, instead of just giving it.

_____ Like

Comment:

May 17
2012

This is not deep n it rhymes. U won't receive, if u don't believe.

_____ Like

Comment:

2013
The enemy wants to see if your light affliction will cause u to praise God less, but God wants to see if u will praise him the more.

_____ Like

Comment:

2016
God is love and there's nothing artificial about it.

_____ Like

Comment:

May 18
2012
One of the greatest demonstrations of love is to "love ur enemies."

_____ Like

Comment:

2014
In all your busyness, you have remained grateful.

_____ Like

Comment:

2016
Make your words count.

_____ Like

Comment:

2017

You can do it now, because you're wiser and stronger.

_____ Like

Comment:

May 19

2016

Be careful not to lose sight of what's really important in life, by being busy with things that really aren't that important. Prioritizing is key today.

_____ Like

Comment:

May 20

2013

For all the preparation you do, you can't fail.

_____ Like

Comment:

2014

If you walk looking back at your past, be sure that you will stumble over your future. If you pray, prepare and practice, you will perfectly, perform your purpose.

_____ Like

Comment:

2015

My son asked for some pie. I said, you just ate. He says, that food has already digested. I say, what is digested? He says, when food goes all through your body. Guess who taught him that? Smh

_____ Like

Comment:

2016

Do something to make your heart say, "thank you."Eat rightExercise Easy day (reduce stress)You deserve it!

_____ Like

Comment:

2017

You are waiting for it to come to you and it is waiting for you to come to it. Smh

_____ Like

Comment:

May 21
2012

It may look dismal, but u r not alone n the fire. Be encouraged.

_____ Like

Comment:

2013

I know why I'm here. I know why I'm fighting. I know I belong to God through Jesus.

_____ Like

Comment:

2014

Sometimes we want people to give us what they don't have and we refrain from giving them what they need. Love somebody today.

_____ Like

Comment:

May 22

2011

while observing some kids on the playground today playing the "dookey touch", one of the kids said, "when I count to 10 u r going to get the dairrhea touch" and I thought, my how times have change.

_____ Like

Comment:

2012

- Finish class last night. One more to go. This is my year!

_____ Like

Comment:

- What the Lord is doing n ur life is a marvelous thing.

_____ Like

Comment:

2013

- Goshen woke up this morning asking, "dad where my drumsticks."May you wake up too asking for your tools to fulfill ur purpose in the earth.

  _____ Like

Comment:

- Goshen told me I'm missing a tooth. I told him that was a gap.

  _____ Like

Comment:

2014

Ever give someone advice? You knew it was good advice, but they didn't follow the advice. Now you know how God feels.

_____ Like

Comment:

2017

If you want to focus, so you can get things done, I suggest a timer.

_____ Like

Comment:

May 23
2012

Have a M.A.D. (make a difference) attitude today.

_____ Like

Comment:

2013

Don't be distracted by the whispers of people, some of them are whispering prayers for you.

_____ Like

Comment:

2014

Have you counted the cost and is it worth it?

_____ Like

Comment:

2016

Mark 4:34 b, but when he was alone with own disciples, he explained everything. Don't you want Jesus to get you alone and explain everything?

_____ Like

Comment:

May 24
2011

Teach me oh Lord.

_____ Like

Comment:

2012
- It's about u today.

U say, "I would, if." IF = Ignore the Future

_____ Like

Comment:

- Just peeped in my son's room to check on him. He says, "get out my house." Don't u think that's a little too hard?

_____ Like

Comment:

2017

It's not a lot, but it's something and it's better than nothing.

_____ Like

Comment:

May 25
2011

I am grateful.

_____ Like

Comment:

2013

Just walked the stage, sure felt good! — at The Baltimore Convention Center.

_____ Like

Comment:

2016

Your emotions must be in check or you will go to a place where you can't come back.

_____ Like

Comment:

2017

You're not to fix everything around you that's broken, some situations will get better on their own.

_____ Like

Comment:

May 26
2015

When you get some good news, you ought to rejoice. I'll take a moment and rejoice.

_____ Like

Comment:

2017

You are a fierce (very strong or intense) prayer warrior and the enemy is surely afraid of you.

_____ Like

Comment:

May 27
2013
You just woke up and the world just became a better place.
_____ Like
Comment:

2014
I'm concerned more about my concerns of me, than your concerns of me.
_____ Like
Comment:

2016
Check out an excerpt from Chapter 4 of my new book out soon."All Those Bottles"I
never really understood much about the game of "Tunk," just knew people were very
competitive. They would play hours of games, then all of a sudden, bottles would
come on the table. They were clear bottles, dark bottles, brown bottles, and tall
bottles on the table. There were all kinds of bottles on that table.
_____ Like
Comment:

May 28
2012
Stop trying to convince them. Who u r will be revealed in time.
_____ Like
Comment:

2013

How hard can it be to trust in The Lord with all your heart and lean not to your own understanding? Proverbs 3:5

_____ Like

Comment:

2014

You can choose to stop placing reminders of your past on your calendar and start making appointments with your future on your calendar.

_____ Like

Comment:

May 29

2012

If u r holding on to it trying to figure out what purpose it serves, u can probably give it away.

_____ Like

Comment:

2013

U say, "I'm going to be successful." That's why u are so determined n focused. I like that about you!

_____ Like

Comment:

2014

Look at you and all that you have. You earned it and you deserve more.

_____ Like

Comment:

May 30
2013

Minister to someone today. You have power in your tongue.

_____ Like

Comment:

2014

You don't want to eat in the car anymore. Pull over and eat on the side of the car. When you have a preschooler, be prepared to clean often.

_____ Like

Comment:

May 31
2011

Why is one year old turning on a laptop?

_____ Like

Comment:

2012

Share ur gift with us please. We've been waiting so long.

_____ Like

Comment:

Big Marv what's up? I know u saw that Avengers joint, but u know u were a super-hero before all those cats. By the way, u save any of those comic books?

_____ Like

Comment:

2013

U have a lopsided view of me because u haven't heard my side.

_____ Like

Comment:

2016

- A new day can be a new opportunity, if you are willing to step out there. Fear is far from you.

_____ Like

Comment:

- Movie date! — checked in to Regal Cinemas Hunt Valley 12 with Shawanda Clark-McCray.

_____ Like

Comment:

CHAPTER 6
June

June 1
2012
Don't be afraid to step out there. U can do it through faith in God n da name of Jesus.

_____ Like

Comment:

2013
The chains that use to bind me have been removed. I can rejoice!

_____ Like

Comment:

2016
One day you will believe more in yourself than you believe in others.

_____ Like

Comment:

June 2
2014

Make money and get paid, but make an impact and a difference.

_____ Like

Comment:

June 3
2014

When you think you have it going on, you won't be alone with those thoughts if you really got it going on.

_____ Like

Comment:

2015

You have a will, so use it.

_____ Like

Comment:

June 4
2011

Sometimes the only explanation was we were just lazy, no other excuse. Today I will be steadfast.

_____ Like

Comment:

2013

My father taught me, "son never be n a hurry to go through the light once it turns green." He saved me from a many accidents. Hesitate to be mean, but be quick to be kind.

_____ Like

Comment:

2014

Want to do the new, but will have to finish the old. Be a completer (new word).

_____ Like

Comment:

2015

May the Joy of the Lord be with you and me today.

_____ Like

Comment:

June 5

2012

Don't be afraid to step out there. U can do it through faith in God n da name of Jesus.

_____ Like

Comment:

2013

That was yesterday, what are you going to do today?"Give us June 5th, 2013 our daily bread." - Matthew 6:11

_____ Like

Comment:

2014

Invest in a timer, so you can devote time to your task and goals in life. I can't live without one.

_____ Like

Comment:

2016

You don't cry over spilled milk because later on you'll have some ice cream.
In the midst of your disappointments, you have successes.

_____ Like

Comment:

2017

You will get stronger in God when you hang out in the gym (presence) of God.

_____ Like

Comment:

June 6
2013

- Hours of watching tv does not equal a disciplined life. The people you are watching are fulfilling their goals.
_____ Like
Comment:

- Learn to keep ur word or shut ur mouth.
_____ Like
Comment:

2014

Today I thought, I don't mind ironing as long as I have a good iron. The same should be true about giving, I don't mind giving as long as I have a good heart.
_____ Like
Comment:

2016

Someone quit smoking.
_____ Like
Comment:

2017

You would give it, if you had it. May you get it, so you can give it.
_____ Like
Comment:

June 7
2011
A new day. I have a chance to live it a little better than the day before.

_____ Like

Comment:

2013
God said to me, "I showed you my love and you know that I love you, so walk in my love today. Hold your head up. Put a smile on your face and love others."

_____ Like

Comment:

2016
You're not that bad because you were made in God's image and his likeness. Genesis 1:27New King James Version (NKJV)27 So God created man in His own image; in the image of God He created him; male and female He created them. Behind those pimples and adipose tissue is a beautiful being.

_____ Like

Comment:

2017
- It will take a lot more than that to break our relationship, because I'm forgiving.

_____ Like

Comment:

- No texting and walking, I believe it has led to many broken phones.
_____ Like
Comment:

June 8
2012
The water is cold n deep, but I'm getting out the boat.
_____ Like
Comment:

2016
Look at you, doing big things. I'm so proud of you.
_____ Like
Comment:

2017
I'm so excited. I will be hanging out with my sister Lucille McCray-Pinkney and my brother Lewis Neal at the movie later today.
_____ Like
Comment:

June 9
2011
At the end of the day, what will u be able to say.
_____ Like
Comment:

2014

Look at your efforts before you complain about your results.

_____ Like

Comment:

2015

Will the Lord find you faithful?

_____ Like

Comment:

2016

You bear the name of Christ, so don't be ashamed, instead rejoice.

_____ Like

Comment:

2017

It's about to turn for your good.

_____ Like

Comment:

June 10
2013

- I see my family this morning, but I won't see then again to much later.

  _____ Like

Comment:

- Obedience is better than sacrifice and family is your first ministry. What a toss up?

_____ Like

Comment:

2014

Would you please hang in there just a little longer? Our change is about to come and we are going to dance together.

_____ Like

Comment:

June 11

2013

Don't worry about folks talking of your past, instead be happy for the ones praying for your future.

I can't make u love me, but if u choose, that's different n better.

_____ Like

Comment:

2014

How many of us would get in a car and go for a ride not knowing when we would stop or where we was going? That's what happens when you use drugs and alcohol.

_____ Like

Comment:

2017

You are not a failure.

_____ Like

Comment:

June 12
2012

God wants me happy.

_____ Like

Comment:

2013

The most feared and revered person on the planet is the person who knows why they are here.

_____ Like

Comment:

2014

Apologizing and forgiving, two words that are inseparable.

_____ Like

Comment:

2017

You are a success.

_____ Like

Comment:

June 13
2013
Don't be in such a hurry soldier that u forget to put on the "whole armor."
_____ Like
Comment:

2017
- It's not your source, but a channel to your source.
_____ Like
Comment:

- In order for me to speak well, I must know well.
_____ Like
Comment:

- I'm in a writing mode as demonstrated by the multiple posts today. I want to share something with writers:1. The book you never write is the story that will never be told. 2. When I finished my books, a part of me was released and it's a feeling that's hard to describe. It's like a message had been delivered and I felt complete. 3. Your book(s) will outlive you. 4. You will never know the impact you had on a person because of the words you placed on paper. 5. Nobody can write your book, but a lot of people can read it and be enriched.
_____ Like
Comment:

June 14
2013

- You're good. it's always better if another person brags bout u than u urself. Proverbs 27:21 just did it for u.
  _____ Like
Comment:

- U r supposed to study the Word like a text book from school.
  _____ Like
Comment:

- Don't get upset when it fails, what was ur plan?
  _____ Like
Comment:

June 15
2012

It's never gonna be the same because of u. Give God the glory.
_____ Like
Comment:

2016

For all the time and energy I'll spend to undo the wrong, I'm better off doing that which is right.
_____ Like
Comment:

2017

The "fire" on you is not age dependent.

_____ Like

Comment:

June 16
2013

Promised Goshen swimming. I came home, but he was sleeping, but I really wanted to keep my promise. He wakes up at 6:10 n says "dad we goin' swimming." we rush to the YMCA n swim for 15 minutes. Glad I could keep my promise. "Happy Integrity Day" to all the men who keep their word.

_____ Like

Comment:

2014

If you are being spiritually fed at your church, support the ministry with your time, money and talents.

_____ Like

Comment:

2017

If you a find a way to laugh today, it won't seem so hard.

_____ Like

Comment:

June 17
2011
"Green Lantern" - very good, action packed.

_____ Like

Comment:

2013
Whatever u do today, don't be lazy.

_____ Like

Comment:

2014
You love God, then loving me is possible.

_____ Like

Comment:

2015
I believe people can change.

_____ Like

Comment:

2016

You could spend your money wisely or foolishly, but at the end of the day you will have to give an account. Invest in learning how to manage money, watch YouTube or get a book. It's time to do something new.

Life is complex, so try to simplify.

_____ Like

Comment:

June 18
2013

- I don't tell u how pretty you are Shawanda, because you are beautiful.

_____ Like

Comment:

- Reduce your time with the people and get rid of the things that you have to ponder, why are they in your life.

_____ Like

Comment:

2014

I'm just curious, should a four year old be able to call his dad's cell phone?

_____ Like

Comment:

June 19
2011
Happy Father God Day. 1 John 3: 1 See what great love the Father has lavished on us, that we should be called children of God! New International Version (NIV)
_____ Like
Comment:

2013
When you pray, the first change that place is in you.1 Thessalonians 5:1717 pray continually,
_____ Like
Comment:

2014
You are a significant person. Never take yourself for granted.
_____ Like
Comment:

June 20
2011
My future looks brighter than my past, so I will focus on my future.
_____ Like
Comment:

2012

Last night my son told me the guitar was looking at him n he could not sleep, so I slept next to the guitar. Kids say the darndest things.

_____ Like

Comment:

2013

Hear the instructions, understand the instructions, then follow the instructions.

_____ Like

Comment:

2014

Why wouldn't The Lord talk to you? You talk to him. That would be so rude.

_____ Like

Comment:

2017

There is nothing preventing you from praying.

_____ Like

Comment:

June 21

2011

U have to go on in spite of.

_____ Like

Comment:

2013

Whatever I do today, I will always praise my God through Jesus.

_____ Like

Comment:

2016

- You would step out and do it, if everybody liked it. I guess you'll never do it.

_____ Like

Comment:

- Thankfulness is a good attitude.

_____ Like

Comment:

June 22

June 23
2011
can u learn to do without?

_____ Like

Comment:

2014
So good to be out of college. I celebrate on Mondays, sometimes all by myself.

_____ Like

Comment:

2016
How many minutes go by before you touch your phone and how many days go by before you touch your Bible?God is a jealous God.

_____ Like

Comment:

June 24
2013
You can do it. Don't let anyone tell you you can't.

_____ Like

Comment:

2014
I have replaced the word tomorrow for the word today. Today sounds better.

_____ Like

Comment:

2014

Save for your rainy day, it will come.

_____ Like

Comment:

2017

Go ahead and do it, what do you have to lose?

_____ Like

Comment:

June 25
2012

It's ok to use ur alarm to prepare for God's presence. Because of my integrity you uphold me and set me in your presence forever. (Psalm 41:12 NIV)

_____ Like

Comment:

2013

- There's a group of muscles to say ur going to do it, but there's another group to do it. Same brain controls them both.

_____ Like

Comment:

- Swimming with Big Goshen, what a pastime.

_____ Like

Comment:

2014

Sometimes people can be mean and nasty, but you can be loving and kind.

_____ Like

Comment:

2016

Trying to choose my title, need some help, which one you like?1. "Valuable, You're Too Good to be Addicted"2. "Valuable, You're Too Good to be Addicted to Alcohol and Drugs"I say alcohol and drugs instead of alcohol or drugs, because alcohol is a drug, but some people don't think so.

_____ Like

Comment:

June 26
2012

Last week a salesman ask me could he Interest me in his product. I said I'm too busy. He said u don't walk like ur busy. Offended yes, but I learned something. Walk purposefully.

_____ Like

Comment:

2013

U got to do what u post. That goes for me too.

_____ Like

Comment:

2014

I'm asking you if you believe in me, when I should be asking do I believe in me?

_____ Like

Comment:

June 27
2013

What do u stand to gain if u put it in your body?
I'm hungry. I'm beginning to taste victory.

_____ Like

Comment:

2014

This morning a bird was in the wood stove trapped. I heard him flapping and opened the door. The bird flew around, then found the door and flew up to the sky. I thought to myself, that's what I will do now that I'm free. I'll believe I can fly.

_____ Like

Comment:

2016

I'm talking to myself, "Joe, don't be anxious."

_____ Like

Comment:

June 28
2012

John 9:35 -Jesus asked the once blind man who was kicked out the temple, "do you believe in the Son of God."It's not what has happened or happening to you, do u believe in him?

_____ Like

Comment:

2013

I am not ashamed of the gospel. Romans 1:16a

_____ Like

Comment:

2017

A credit card is a fee card. It is not a free card.

_____ Like

Comment:

June 29
2012

Have a great weekend n they asked u to do it bc you r Capable Available No-nonsense (CAN)

_____ Like

Comment:

2015
Don't just let the day happen, plan your day.
_____ Like
Comment:

2016
Your passion separates you from the rest. Find your passion.
_____ Like
Comment:

2017
It's not in your hands. It's in God's hands and that's better.
_____ Like
Comment:

June 30
2016
It hasn't always been easy, but you are determined to succeed. That's what make you special!
_____ Like
Comment:

2017
Peter (Acts 12) and Paul (Acts 16) were miraculously sprung forth from prison. Why wouldn't your God free you from your bondage?
_____ Like
Comment:

CHAPTER 7
July

July 1
2011
Transformers "rocks". I predict it will be the biggest grossing movie thus far this summer.

_____ Like

Comment:

2013
shall walk and not faint. Naw, I shall run again. Better yet, I shall fly like an eagle.

_____ Like

Comment:

2014
Thanks to the assistance from Goshen the family newsletters have been mailed. He put his special touch on each envelope.

_____ Like

Comment:

2015

The wait is over. The wheels have turned. Finally it is happening before my very eyes and I'm most thankful!Don't get weary in doing good, but in due season you shall reap, if you faint not. Galatians 6:9

_____ Like

Comment:

2016

I'm serious. Become a student of the Word of God. Designate 10 - 15 minutes minimum to read, then learn to study. You will never be the same.

_____ Like

Comment:

July 2

2011

Sometimes it's good to just relax.

_____ Like

Comment:

2013

Family time is a wise investment.

_____ Like

Comment:

2014

Don't let nothing interfere with your prayer life. No FB, gym, food, tv, people or things. I mean nothing.

_____ Like

Comment:

2016

My child is wild.

_____ Like

Comment:

July 3

2012

The takeaway word from this storm is "power."

_____ Like

Comment:

2013

I would hate to think where I would be without your prayers. Thanks for praying.

_____ Like

Comment:

2014

Don't get mad at folks who live disciplined lives, instead ask them to tell you their secrets.

_____ Like

Comment:

2017

This is a temporary mess and I mean temporary.

_____ Like

Comment:

July 4
2012

Power!

_____ Like

Comment:

2013

Go on. Shake yourself. Square your shoulders back. Lift up your head. You are going to do this time.

_____ Like

Comment:

I smell like a grill, but I'm satisfied, my family and I.

_____ Like

Comment:

July 5
2012

Money:

Give, Save, Bills and Self

_____ Like

Comment:

2013

Anyone who has been stealing (such as work time) must steal no longer, but must work, doing something useful with their own hands, that they may have something to share with those in need. Ephesians 4:28New International Version (©2011)

_____ Like

Comment:

2015

Tasha Cobbs sings,"For your glory, I will do anything."I wonder how many of us would do anything for God's glory?

_____ Like

Comment:

2016

I want to say something to really encourage your heart and let you know I want the best for you. I got it! "Good Morning" "Have a great day."

_____ Like

Comment:

2017

How do you do it all without a plan and a planner?

_____ Like

Comment:

July 6
2012
Will u walk or run to him?

_____ Like

Comment:

2017
Oh the blood of Jesus, thank you for the blood.

_____ Like

Comment:

July 7
2015
You want to smack the devil in the mouth? Do good.

_____ Like

Comment:

July 8
2013
I shall not be afraid.

_____ Like

Comment:

It's time to pull out the shoes n celebrate. I mean dancing shoes, Happy Birthday to one of the best leadoff legs in the two mile relay for Baltimore, Troy Dean.

_____ Like

Comment:

2014
If I don't succeed, the first person I'll blame is me.
_____ Like
Comment:

2017
Vacation allows me to reset, refocus and reposition myself for the next chapter of my life.
_____ Like
Comment:

July 9
2011

- 4 things u should do with money. Read this in a children's book. 1 Give some away2 pay your bills/debt3 save some4 buy yourself something
  _____ Like
Comment:

- U keep trying to fit in, supposed u found out that u r an eagle and u r to fly alone.
  _____ Like
Comment:

- It won't always be that way.
  _____ Like
Comment:

2012
U have the time. Don't ponder.
_____ Like
Comment:

2013
My big brother James said it before Nike. James 1:2222 But be doers of the word, and not hearers only, deceiving yourselves. I'll be a doer today.
_____ Like
Comment:

2014
Your hands are not big enough for this one.
_____ Like
Comment:

2016
I don't have a lot of time or money, but I can do something.
Those that remain, remember the slain.
That's my goal, not just in posts, but in a way to bring honor to their names.
_____ Like
Comment:

2017

Life changing message today at DreamLife Worship Center, "Til Debt Do Us Part" on the importance of financial stewardship before and during a relationship from Pastors Kenneth O. Robinson Jr. and Lady Lenyar Sloan-Robinson. It was so good, that all the CDs were sold out, go figure.

_____ Like

Comment:

July 10
2012

I appreciate the power of choices.

_____ Like

Comment:

2013

It was his time. I didn't answer the phone. I held off on talking with wife about our vacation. Nothing was more important. We played football. We boxed. We wrestled. We played on his toy laptop. It was his time.

_____ Like

Comment:

July 11
2012

This summer, get out of this town n take some vacation, u deserve it.

_____ Like

Comment:

2013

U can't take that extra job. U got to fulfill another goal, that will payoff much better. It wasn't much, just some pork chops, corn n string beans, but we were all together as a family.

_____ Like

Comment:

2016

Get a daily life routine and stick to it. Get started with a calendar on the wall with what you will be doing daily, weekly and monthly. No more wasting time.

_____ Like

Comment:

2017

Your prayer life is your "power - filled" life.

_____ Like

Comment:

July 12
2012

Nuthin like breakfast with my son and the Wiggles. "let's have some fun."

_____ Like

Comment:

2013

Will follow after my big brother Joshua when he says, " Only be strong and very courageous" Joshua 1:7aI'll be strong and very courageous today.

_____ Like

Comment:

2017

I know you want to be successful, but do you have the time to be successful?
We are good and we're only getting better.

_____ Like

Comment:

July 13

2012

If I love God with all my heart, soul, mind n strength, that's how I can love you too. Mark 12:29-31

_____ Like

Comment:

2016

A door is shut, but God opens a bigger one, the first door had you stooping down to get through. Don't be afraid of the bigger.

_____ Like

Comment:

2017

The stock value of your "time" has increased.

_____ Like

Comment:

July 14
2014

Two of my favorites:1. Hanging with my wife. 2. Seeing movies.

_____ Like

Comment:

2015

An elderly gentleman said to me this morning, "Don't have a workout, instead have a fun out."

_____ Like

Comment:

2017

I feel on "fire" today.

_____ Like

Comment:

July 15
2013

Tenacity to me means = moving forward to your goal in spite of how u feel or think.

_____ Like

Comment:

2014

Work harder and talk lesser.

_____ Like

Comment:

2016

After you have served your purpose, please sit down. Jesus did, Luke 22:69

_____ Like

Comment:

2015

Rock climbing is only the beginning of their future achievements. Im hanging out with "boys on the move" Goshen, Dante' and Makai (son and great, great nephews).

_____ Like

Comment:

July 16
2013

- FB wants u to share how u r feeling. Post, post, post. There is a book, a story, a message n u. Many people like ur post, but will never tell u publicly, but don't let that stop u.

_____ Like

Comment:

- $16 carwash included tires cleaned n air freshener. $10 carwash excluded tires cleaned n air freshener. Saved $6 bc wheels are cleaned while the cars go through n I had an air freshener. Inquire about the difference?
  _____ Like
  Comment:

- Complete ur goal (s) when u get the urge, if u wait u can get constipated, then nothing will happen for u.
  _____ Like
  Comment:

- Ur rest is important.
  _____ Like
  Comment:

2017
One of our responsibilities is to enjoy this life we have been given.
_____ Like
Comment:

July 17
2011
Not enough for me to hear the Word of God, I must do the Word of God.
_____ Like
Comment:

2012

Whatever u have become is good, but there is so much more to you.
This Sweet Potato Pie is the joint — at Johns Hopkins Hospital.

_____ Like

Comment:

2013

A miracle happened n prayer service tonight. A great testimony is forthcoming.

_____ Like

Comment:

2014

We say "Lord I won't fear and I won't worry." What about, "Lord I won't gossip or I won't hate."

_____ Like

Comment:

2017

You have more time than you realize.

_____ Like

Comment:

July 18
2013

Everybody should have a sister, like my sister Lucille. She is a blessing.

_____ Like

Comment:

2014

I was asked to give advice to someone overcoming drug addiction or alcoholism. I said, "never give up and don't stay down if you fall as people will walk on you."

_____ Like

Comment:

2017

I got to be more healthier. Three of the top preventable deaths are:1. Smoking cigarettes2. Overeating/obesity3. Alcohol consumptionI encourage you all to be aware, get information and seek help. You don't need to leave earth before your time and then say, "God called your number." We all can be more healthier.

_____ Like

Comment:

July 19
2013

You have time to pray.

_____ Like

Comment:

🙏

2016

Your assignment requires much prayer.

_____ Like

Comment:

2017

When you hear the word "methadone," what comes to your mind?

_____ Like

Comment:

July 20

2012

What is wisdom, if u don't use it.

_____ Like

Comment:

2016

Somebody is always watching you.

_____ Like

Comment:

2017

Focusing on the solution - the problem = good results

_____ Like

Comment:

July 21

2014

No more time wasting. Now it's time to get it done.

_____ Like

Comment:

2016
There's was a time I use to be afraid of you, but now your opinion fuels me to be better.

_____ Like

Comment:

2017
There's a lot going on in the White House, but America stay alert and focused.

_____ Like

Comment:

July 22
2013
Make your mark in the history books, one step at a time.

_____ Like

Comment:

2014
I don't have to get it all done today, but eventually.

_____ Like

Comment:

2015
You have gone on to a new level. The things that use to upset you, don't upset you anymore.

_____ Like

Comment:

2016

Today I got a glimpse of my tomorrow; I know tomorrow is not promised, but I'm excited.

You don't have to hold on to your past anymore, there are others who will do it for you.

_____ Like

Comment:

2017

- I don't want a bunch of degrees, if I can't help my fellow brother or sister.

_____ Like

Comment:

- It's not that serious.

_____ Like

Comment:

- I've come to realize, just like the natural seasons have a beginning and end, so are the seasons in our life. We are never "seasonless." (new word - living life in no season)

_____ Like

Comment:

July 23
2013

I applaud all the people who have to clean bathrooms.

_____ Like

Comment:

2012

We did it. Last class. Last paper. Finished the Baccalaureate Program at Notre Dame of Maryland University. We are so excited. — with Tyra's Page at Outback Steakhouse - Perry Hall.

_____ Like

Comment:

2013

I am passionate about helping people with drug addiction, HIV/AIDS and mental illness. As the sole owner of Education For The Community, LLC an outreach business founded to provide education for the community, I will be in downtown Baltimore talking about the "Health Dangers of Alcohol Use" today. Schedule your lecture now for your school, agency or place of business by going to www.mccraylectures.com

July 24
2013

I'm getting it done.

_____ Like

Comment:

2017

Do what you can do within your power (ability) such as:1. Eat right2. Get good sleep3. Exercise4. Manage your money5. Reduce stressThen, you can leave the rest to God, but let us do our part.

_____ Like

Comment:

July 25
2013

Some things are over and never to return. Thank God.

_____ Like

Comment:

2014

My son has taught, that being a father means, to be loving and present.

_____ Like

Comment:

2016

It's a sacrifice now, but you are going to love the results later.

_____ Like

Comment:

2017

This was on my heart this morning and it was in my daily reading. Be blessed. "Do not be overcome by evil, but overcome evil with good." Romans 12:21 (NIV)

_____ Like

Comment:

July 26
2012

U r being tried bc the best is about to be revealed.

_____ Like

Comment:

2013

It's going to take place for u, just u wait n see.

_____ Like

Comment:

2017

In my mind and in my heart, I love the Lord today.

_____ Like

Comment:

July 27
2012

Some people r past, so stop involving them n ur future. Be free.

_____ Like

Comment:

2015

Sometimes you can spend your energy and time on things that really don't matter. May you have the wisdom to say no and mean it.

_____ Like

Comment:

2016

A happy wife is a happy life.

_____ Like

Comment:

July 28
2016

1 Corinthians 7:3-4 The husband should fulfill his marital duty to his wife, and likewise the wife to her husband. The wife does not have authority over her own body but yields it to her husband. In the same way, the husband does not have authority over his own body but yields it to his wife. (New international Version)

_____ Like

Comment:

2017

It's called an "extra-marital affair," do you really have time for the "extra?" Give the extra to your spouse instead, smh!

_____ Like

Comment:

July 29
2013
Just one Word from God can change ur life forever, may u receive that Word today.

_____ Like

Comment:

2016
I can't afford it right now, but I am going to get it.

_____ Like

Comment:

2017
Doors shut in your face is an indication you've been knocking. Keep knocking and "the door" shall be open.

_____ Like

Comment:

July 30
2013
I've been trying to figure you out n I think I got it. You are an original.

_____ Like

Comment:

July 31
2013
I'm not totally convince by your actions that u really want what u say.

_____ Like

Comment:

CHAPTER 8
August

August 1
2013
I'll consider the finer things in life.
_____ Like
Comment:

2016
Some people can't tell who you are from your posts; they haven't received the memo that you have grown.
_____ Like
Comment:

2017
You can't "erase" the past, but you can "write" your future.
_____ Like
Comment:

BMI 25.47. I'm rolling.

_____ Like

Comment:

August 2
2012

Not that I have done it all right, yet I press.

_____ Like

Comment:

2013

In Jesus name be fortified.

_____ Like

Comment:

2016

Your enemies are astonished at how you keep surviving after all those attacks. You have the greater one inside of you. 1 John 4:4.

_____ Like

Comment:

2017

I have to stay positive. I will not get far in the negative.

_____ Like

Comment:

August 3
2017
No doubt we are making an effort, but we have to stretch out some more.

_____ Like

Comment:

August 4
2017
You're supposed to be a Christian" and that you are and a faithful one too.

_____ Like

Comment:

It's never a convenient time to be successful.

_____ Like

Comment:

August 5
2013
It's cheaper, but is it better.

_____ Like

Comment:

August 6
2017

May your awake hours this week be productive and meaningful. Try to minimize wasting more than two hours in a given day.

_____ Like

Comment:

August 7
2013

Be free to do u today.

_____ Like

Comment:

2017

While you wait, continue to prepare for your greater, it's coming.

_____ Like

Comment:

August 8
2013

Will celebrate my wife even more, it's her birthday.

_____ Like

Comment:

2017

Would you help me celebrate Shawanda Clark-McCray's birthday! She is beautiful, intelligent and caring. May her day be filled with an abundance of love.— with Shawanda Clark-McCray.

_____ Like

Comment:

I was trying not to post today, but I can't help myself. Each day is a process of putting ourselves together. May all the pieces come together for something good today for you.

_____ Like

Comment:

August 9
2011

I have passed the test. I'm ready for the next level blessing.

_____ Like

Comment:

2013

Shawanda said she enjoyed her birthday.

_____ Like

Comment:

2016
Learn to love prayer and you will walk in a power you have never known.
_____ Like
Comment:

2017
You and I will talk less and do more.
_____ Like
Comment:

August 10

August 11
2015
Keep it moving. No time to sit still or be complacent.

_____ Like

Comment:

2016
It is said, "you don't get everything you want in life," but at least strive for it, you never know how close you'll get.

_____ Like

Comment:

2017
I have changed my diet in preparation for the greater because I know it's coming.

_____ Like

Comment:

August 12
2013
Nothing shall stop me from fulfilling my purpose.

_____ Like

Comment:

2015

You can cry over spilled milk, but eventually it will dry up and then what are you going to do?

_____ Like

Comment:

2016

If it's going to get done, you have to do it, because you can't afford to pay anybody else to do it for you.

_____ Like

Comment:

August 13

2011

It's about getting started n the race and finishing. Think I'll keep running my race.

_____ Like

Comment:

2012

All you can do is your best. Have a Do Your Best Day.

_____ Like

Comment:

2013

Step by step you are going to reach ur goal, just don't look back at the past.

_____ Like

Comment:

2015

I tried to be a lot of things growing up, but becoming a Christian was the best thing I could've ever done.

_____ Like

Comment:

2016

I wouldn't be the man I am today, if it wasn't for the 15 year fine leadership example of my Pastor Kenneth O. Robinson Jr.

_____ Like

Comment:

August 14

2012

Sometimes I post to encourage others, but n fact I'm really encouraging myself.

_____ Like

Comment:

2013

Step by step you are going to reach ur goal, just don't look back at the past.

_____ Like

Comment:

2015

Know this, if you hear a voice in your head or your heart suggesting to you to pray or to pray longer, it's not the devil.

_____ Like

Comment:

2016

Everybody will not be able to go to your next destination with you and don't feel sad, it's just the way it is.

Sometimes you just have to remind yourself of who you are.

_____ Like

Comment:

August 15

2011

When no one else believes n u, God does, that's reassuring.

_____ Like

Comment:

2012

Incredible sleep, even in the midst of the storm, but why am I trying to turn on lights when there is no power.

_____ Like

Comment:

2013

I can write my best when it's quiet. What about you?

_____ Like

Comment:

2017

Memorizing scriptures is work that will have long lasting benefits.

_____ Like

Comment:

August 16
2012

Stop getting mad with people who have no capacity for you, you have outgrown them. Instead seek out people who have room for you.

_____ Like

Comment:

2013

Last day of the work week, so go out in style.

_____ Like

Comment:

2016

I'm determined to win!

_____ Like

Comment:

2017

Powerful message tonight at Bible Study from Kenneth O. Robinson Jr., God did something new and fresh in our midst. I encourage you all to attend Dreamlife Worship Center; 4111 Deer Park Drive: Randallstown, Maryland 21133Wednesdays 7 pmSundays 8 am (August only)Sundays 10 am

_____ Like

Comment:

August 17
2012

It's ok to say, thank you Jesus.

_____ Like

Comment:

You know what needs to be done. Get up and do it.

_____ Like

Comment:

As I watched these olympics, I look back on running with one of the greatest runners that came through Mervo, Rickey Lonza Meekins. Thanks for your example!

_____ Like

Comment:

You are in the right place at the right time. Something new n fresh for u.

_____ Like

Comment:

2015

You've come this far. You might as well go all the way.

_____ Like

Comment:

2016

Laziness is not one of your strong points.

_____ Like

Comment:

August 18

2017

What good is a great idea, that you are afraid to act upon, don't ask for it, if you don't believe you deserve it.

_____ Like

Comment:

August 19

2013

Got to keep moving in the right direction, no u turns.

_____ Like

Comment:

August 20
2012
Oh oh, oh oh back to work I go.

_____ Like

Comment:

2013
Don't give your time away anymore unless you have a purpose to it.

_____ Like

Comment:

August 21
2012
You already know what you should be doing, then what's the problem.
Get with it.

_____ Like

Comment:

2013
It'll get done, slow n steady.

_____ Like

Comment:

2017
You have a few people that agree with what you are doing, that's all you need.

_____ Like

Comment:

August 22
2011
This is not meant to be deep or spiritual, but there is greatness n u. Discovered it soon.

_____ Like

Comment:

I applaud every single parent who has given or who is giving their best to raise a child. I am clapping for u.

_____ Like

Comment:

2012
One day food won't be so important.

_____ Like

Comment:

2013
Apologize, that was mean.

_____ Like

Comment:

2016
Finish reading or writing the chapter. The story has to be heard.

_____ Like

Comment:

August 23
2012
Be prepared, prompt, prayerful, positive and most of all be powerful.

_____ Like

Comment:

2013
I will serve The Lord.

_____ Like

Comment:

2015
You say, "I don't have time to pray or read the Word of God," but you have time to read this post.

Jesus was daily teaching in the temple days before his betrayal and death. Luke 21:37 - 38How many of us will continue to do God's work, days before our test?

_____ Like

Comment:

2016
I went back to reading, "How to Study the Bible for Yourself" by Tim LaHaye. If you desire, like me, to be stronger in the Lord, this book is a must read.

_____ Like

Comment:

August 24
2012
Did u ever think u would be doing what u r doing, living this way n having these things?It's amazing what God has done for u.

_____ Like

Comment:

2016
There are more people who like and pray for you than you think.

_____ Like

Comment:

2017
We can always get better at what we do.

_____ Like

Comment:

August 25
2015
You are full of purpose. Walk in your purpose today.

_____ Like

Comment:

2017

In my heart, I felt something good was going to happen for me today. Well, I cooked some fish and had my greens, then it happened. I went outside to the trunk of my car and there it was, something good. It arrived at the exact moment I opened the door, it was the ice cream truck. I knew all day something good was going to happen for me today.

_____ Like

Comment:

August 26
2011

It matters more to me what God thinks about me than what people think about me. Be free today.

_____ Like

Comment:

2013

Sometimes you can be dissatisfied, get angry and change.

_____ Like

Comment:

2016

There are people suffering with alcohol and substance use disorders, but help is on the way.

_____ Like

Comment:

August 27
2011

None of us r perfect, don't beat ur self up so bad. Been there, done that. Sometimes our blows hurt the most. Don't sweat it.

_____ Like

Comment:

Saw "The Help", never cried so much watching a movie.

_____ Like

Comment:

2012

Some r for u and some r not, which ones will u focus on?

_____ Like

Comment:

2013

My wife is beautiful.

_____ Like

Comment:

2016

When it's comes to a problem, you can watch and do nothing or you can watch and try to fix it. It all starts with an observation.

_____ Like

Comment:

August 28
2012
Aren't you glad today that you r more considerate of your words and actions.

_____ Like

Comment:

2013
My son is courageous. He told me Sunday in church, "dad I'm not afraid of nothing."

_____ Like

Comment:

2017
May you and I continue to do things in excellence.

_____ Like

Comment:

August 29
2012
Thanks God, for the restoration project called, "Me." You have ur work cut out for you, but u r the master builder.

_____ Like

Comment:

2013
Don't walk fast or jog, but run this race.

_____ Like

Comment:

2016

You don't have to fake it anymore. You are anointed and gifted to do what you do.

_____ Like

Comment:

August 30

2011

I feel like goin' on.

2012

May God's light be be so bright in you today that people can't recognize it's you.

_____ Like

Comment:

Fleshly subjection is a spiritual thing, stop trying in your one might. Tap into God's power.

_____ Like

Comment:

2013

Don't have much to say, but I have much to do. All hard work brings a profit, but mere talk leads only to poverty. (Proverbs 14:23 NIV)

_____ Like

Comment:

2015

Goshen's first day of school.

_____ Like

Comment:

August 31
2011

R u talking too much. "he who has knowledge spares his words, And a man of understanding is of a calm spirit. (Proverbs 17:27 NKJV)

Get on with ur goal. What r u waiting for. It's ur time. If u don't do it, who else will.

_____ Like

Comment:

2012

U don't have time for other people's foolishness, stay focused, don't be distracted bc u r going places.

_____ Like

Comment:

2015

Unfriend procrastination and request to be friends with determination.

_____ Like

Comment:

CHAPTER 9
September

September 1
2016
Isn't it upsetting when you can't find something, only to realize you didn't put it back where it belonged. The Word of God is the same way, you can't find the Word for your situation because you didn't put it back where it belongs, in your heart and mind.

_____ Like

Comment:

September 2
2011
Want to improve ur memory? Paste important things on your calendar in your mobile phone and set it to remind u daily, weekly or monthly. U will be surprised how well ur memory will improve. Folks use their mobile phones a lot, why not get the most out of it.

_____ Like

Comment:

I would've rather u showed me ur love n never told me than to have told me but never showed me.

_____ Like

Comment:

2015

I was just thinking, if God would inspire dozens of people to write about his relationship with mankind. What are you inspired to do, so that the world could see?

_____ Like

Comment:

I'm learning to be a better listener. That means it's not all about me.

_____ Like

Comment:

You are never alone because God is with you. It might look like it, it might even feel like it, but you are never alone.

_____ Like

Comment:

September 3
2011

As a parent when u call your child(ren) bad, r u bad too?

_____ Like

Comment:

I think when u r a giver, u will always receive. Look at Oprah, Bill Gates, God and U. For God so loved that he gave.... John 3:16a

_____ Like

Comment:

2012

Had an incredible experience at my first meeting with the Black Writers Guild. K. L. Blady published author "The Bum Magnet" blessed me tremendously. If u have a book in u, consider joining. BWG@blackwritersguild.org

_____ Like

Comment:

2016

How many of you would do anything to see God's glory?

_____ Like

Comment:

September 4
2012

Get up, get moving and get accomplishments.

_____ Like

Comment:

Many times God has said yes, but we hate the "not right now" part. For example, I'll say yes to my son, but unfortunately, he hears "not right now."

_____ Like

Comment:

2015

You are on a road never traveled before, because you are a trailblazer.

_____ Like

Comment:

2016

Transparent, that's what I'll be.

_____ Like

Comment:

September 5
2011

Hard to live 2 lives, even Superman and Spiderman eventually revealed their true identities.

_____ Like

Comment:

2012

Your plan is of God this time and no one will be able to overthrow it. Acts 5:39Hold ur head up extremely high today.

_____ Like

Comment:

September 6
2011
Not that I have done everything right, but what I am excited about, is that I am in the Will of God. I like that place.

_____ Like

Comment:

2012
Be full of good works today.

_____ Like

Comment:

2016
You're doing all the right things, you just have to wait, it's a process.

_____ Like

Comment:

September 7
2010
We serve a gigantic God.

_____ Like

Comment:

2013
I've been exclusively enjoying wife and son last week in Sandusky, Ohio and this week at home. I will always take some time away to enjoy what matters the most.
_____ Like
Comment:

2015
Being positive means opposing the negative.
_____ Like
Comment:

2016
It's hard to be or to stay negative when you're around positive. It's going to rub off on you.
_____ Like
Comment:

September 8
2014
If you have to crawl before you walk, walk before you run, then you have to run before you fly.
_____ Like
Comment:

2016

Don't keep knocking on the same doors. There are more doors or opportunities for you and me.

_____ Like

Comment:

September 9
2011

Some people we use to play with when we were younger, we can't play with them no more bc they are still playing the same games.

_____ Like

Comment:

2014

This morning Gosh says, "dad let's watch the news,"but 3 minutes later we're watching Nick Jr. Nick Jr. is more entertaining.

_____ Like

Comment:

2016

Walk in the confidence that God is with you.

_____ Like

Comment:

September 10
2012
God is _____.
_____ Like
Comment:

2013
I've been exclusively enjoying wife and son last week in Sandusky, Ohio and this week at home. I will always take some time away to enjoy what matters the most.
_____ Like
Comment:

2014
What would you do if you were not afraid anymore?
_____ Like
Comment:

September 11
2012
Tension is good bc u are able to bounce back today.
_____ Like
Comment:

2013

It's gonna get done because you and I are determined people.

What am I willing to sacrifice for success? What are you wiling to sacrifice for your success? Key word is "willing."

_____ Like

Comment:

2016

Enjoy life, each and every day! Don't let one day go by without getting the most out of it.

_____ Like

Comment:

September 12
2011

U trippin over one or two people not studdin u, when there r 700,000 people n Baltimore, 5 million in Md, 300 million in the USA, 6.5 billion in the world. Get on with ur life n show someone else ur friendly, kind n loving heart.

_____ Like

Comment:

2012

You say, just believe. I say it's difficult. Lord help my unbelief.

_____ Like

Comment:

2013

There's is no God like Jehovah and no brother that sticks closer than Jesus.

_____ Like

Comment:

2016

Eat like you understand your purpose in life.

_____ Like

Comment:

September 13
2011

Voted. Now have to wait to see some new outcomes for the city.

_____ Like

Comment:

When u were younger n got out of school, when u got home after school was that ur snack or dinner? (elementary age)I ate a lot of peanut butter n jelly sandwiches after school. That had to be a snack.

_____ Like

Comment:

2012

U alone saw the vision for ur life. It will comes to past. Habakkuk 2:2

_____ Like

Comment:

Good financial talk with my wife last night. No financial unfaithfulness.
_____ Like
Comment:

2013
How often do u stop to take a deep breathe?
_____ Like
Comment:

2016
I hear my mom's words, "you can do anything you want to do, if you put your mind to it." - Josephine Jordan
_____ Like
Comment:

September 14
2012
They don't like me, so.
_____ Like
Comment:

2015
What shall separate you from the love of God?As for me, nothing shall separate me from the love of God.
_____ Like
Comment:

September 15
2011
Hold ur head up, God is proud of u.

_____ Like

Comment:

2015
You don't have to change, but "Watch Me." I will.

_____ Like

Comment:

September 16
2013
Be faithful to what to what you know is true.

_____ Like

Comment:

September 17
2011
If u remove certain things out of ur way, u don't have to worry about stumbling over them.

_____ Like

Comment:

I think this is powerful. Jesus was confronted with one of the rulers of the synagogue's daughter, who is sick next to death. The ruler name is Jairus and he begs Jesus to come and heal her. Some time passes and information gets to Jesus that the ruler no longer needs to trouble Jesus because, "your daughter is dead." Mark 5:36 says, as soon as Jesus heard the word that was spoken, he said to the ruler of the synagogue, "Do not be afraid; only believe."What are you afraid of, "only believe"

_____ Like

Comment:

2012

Had a problem last night, but I was determined to fix it. Now the water flows smoothly. Be determined to fix all ur problems.

_____ Like

Comment:

2013

"Don't tell the secrets to your strength like Samson did." - Minister Monte Torry

_____ Like

Comment:

2015

After all that preparation, now you are ready for the test. Do well.

_____ Like

Comment:

September 18
2012
I'm well rested and positive.

_____ Like

Comment:

2013
You are going to attract enemies for the kind of life you live.

_____ Like

Comment:

2015
Don't miss out on following your purpose, fooling with people who don't know their purpose in life.

_____ Like

Comment:

2016
Enjoy this life, I am.

_____ Like

Comment:

September 19
2011
I'm shocked n saddened about the news of Calvin Brown's death. What a humble man. U will be missed.

_____ Like

Comment:

2012
I'm trying to show u my love but u r always on FB, the phone, watching TV or eating. Lord I'm never too busy for you.

_____ Like

Comment:

2013
You know you are serious about saving money when u pack lunch for two days.

_____ Like

Comment:

2016
There are people in your life who want to stretch you, but you are so resistant that you easily break. Loosen up and grow.

_____ Like

Comment:

September 20
2011

It is said, the race isn't given to the swift but the one who endures to the end. I think I'll endure.

_____ Like

Comment:

Wonderful dinner. Shake n Bake Chicken, string beans and corn. Will have to do that Shake n Bake again.

_____ Like

Comment:

2012

Have a God day. The world will see the greatest in you today.

_____ Like

Comment:

2013

If you ever lose something important like ur mind, strength or money, when u get it back, please appreciate it this time.

_____ Like

Comment:

September 21
2011
U got to have haters n ur life. They help u have perseverance New International Version (©1984)Not only so, but we also rejoice in our sufferings, because we know that suffering produces perseverance; Romans 5:3

_____ Like

Comment:

2012
Son is going to sleep earlier. More time with my wife. I like that.

_____ Like

Comment:

2016
I want to give a shout to all my nieces and nephews. I wanted to text you all, but it's early. I was just thinking about the adults many of you have become and I'm proud of you all young and old. Love Uncle Joe.

_____ Like

Comment:

Treatment for substance use, dial 211 or call Behavioral Health Systems (410) 637-1900, Monday - Friday 8 am - 5 pm. No insurance or no ID still call.

_____ Like

Comment:

September 22
2016

I'm positioned for increase.

_____ Like

Comment:

September 23
2016

Why are you still in the bed? You have work that must be done.

_____ Like

Comment:

September 24
2011

At the playground today, boys chase the girls n vice versa. They catch each other n throw one another to the ground. Then belts come off n they start chasing one another with belts. I asked what's the name of this game? Young girl says, "it's boys chase the girls." I think we were a little nicer to the girls during my younger days.

_____ Like

Comment:

2013

The sacrifice you are making now is gonna payoff big in your future.

_____ Like

Comment:

September 25
2011
Baltimore Book Festival in Mount Vernon today.

_____ Like

Comment:

2012
One day u will declare that, "you are beautiful and loved."One day that will happen for u, that's my prayer.

_____ Like

Comment:

2013
The Lord speaks good of you.

_____ Like

Comment:

September 26
2011
Some events n life are embarrassing n flat out humiliating, but if u learn from them you'll be a better personBeen there, done that.

_____ Like

Comment:

2012
Count your blessings, bc you have so many.

_____ Like

Comment:

2013
There's greatness in you, but you already knew this.

_____ Like

Comment:

2014
You spewed all of your attacks and they only made me stronger. Thanks for making me better.

_____ Like

Comment:

2015
What good would it be to receive gifts from God or a person, but have no relationship? This has to change.

_____ Like

Comment:

2016
Get a picture in your mind of your dream and feverishly work at achieving it.

_____ Like

Comment:

September 27
2011
Got to eat ur fiber, fruits, vegetables n drink ur water. Bottom line ur bowel movements need to be regular n easy. For more info ask ur medical provider. Don't want problems later in ur life.

_____ Like

Comment:

2012
In spite of me, u still love me God. Who wouldn't serve a God like u.

_____ Like

Comment:

2013
If I would only believe, I do believe.

_____ Like

Comment:

2016
I learned three things from the debate:1. Tell the truth. 2. Be in control of your emotions. 3. Have stamina.

_____ Like

Comment:

Phony people irritate me.

_____ Like

Comment:

September 28
2011
Best advice my brother gave me, "u don't have to comment to everything people say." Lewis Neal.

_____ Like

Comment:

Wonder how long do post stay on FB?

_____ Like

Comment:

2012
So, let me get this. As I think I am, I am. Proverbs 23:7 That's amazing.

_____ Like

Comment:

September 29
2011
I will bask in God's magnificent love today.
Always hold ur head up.

_____ Like

Comment:

September 30
2011
Everybody won't be happy for u but be thankful for the ones who r. Josephine JordanOne of God's wisest women and my mom.

_____ Like

Comment:

2013
There must be one person you can be transparent with?

_____ Like

Comment:

2015
You can't give what don't have, but you can go out and get what you need.

_____ Like

Comment:

2016
I thought of all the reasons I didn't have time to read the Word this morning, then I considered all that was done that the Word would be available for me, so I spent 15 minutes in his Word. His Word is true!

_____ Like

Comment:

CHAPTER 10
October

October 1
2011
After u have paid off the debt, what will be the lesson you have learned.
If u don't learn something through the process, u r bound to repeat the behavior.
Been there, done that.
_____ Like
Comment:

2012
It is 5 am, and I hear a scream, "pizza." It's our son.
I wonder will he remember this request when he awakes.
_____ Like
Comment:

2013
You don't need a title to be a blessing.
U were on ur way to being a burden, but instead, u turned out to be a blessing.
_____ Like
Comment:

2016

You and I must not allow people to treat us anyway. We are children of the King of Kings, so let's act like it.

Life is not a sprint, so pace yourself and run a good race.

_____ Like

Comment:

October 2
2011

It was good for me to be in God's house.

_____ Like

Comment:

2012

_____ Like

Comment:

I don't know how u do it without prayer.

2013

Take a good look at yourself in the mirror, "because u have been fearfully and wonderfully made." (Psalms 139:14 a)

_____ Like

Comment:

October 3
2011
Some say it's not what u say but how u say it. I believe it's what u say too.
Been there, done that.
Will choose my words carefully.

_____ Like

Comment:

2012
If I told u once, I told u twice. There's greatness in you.

_____ Like

Comment:

2013
Thank you for praying for me before I told u my problem.

_____ Like

Comment:

2016
Be observant today, what you're seeking is seeking you too.

_____ Like

Comment:

October 4

2011

Who said u couldn't pray in the car?

_____ Like

Comment:

2012

6 am eating a freezy pop n watching Nick Jr. with our precious son.

_____ Like

Comment:

2013

I can see it coming to past, and it's gonna be sweet.

_____ Like

Comment:

2016

Stay still and know that you and I serve a mighty God, who is able to keep us from falling.

_____ Like

Comment:

2017

I surround myself around great, loving, wise and powerful people and every once in awhile a little of them rubs off on me.

_____ Like

Comment:

October 5
2011
Nobody became successful on their first try.
They tried again, and again and....
_____ Like
Comment:

2012
I am a good steward of the money.
_____ Like
Comment:

October 6
2011
Will not waste time and will not let people waste my time.
_____ Like
Comment:

2016
I keep asking and answering this question, "how bad do you want it?"
"I want it bad," so I keep "pushing on" as my mom use to say.
_____ Like
Comment:

2017

My attitude determines my altitude.

_____ Like

Comment:

October 7

2013

Make it a habit of praising God.

_____ Like

Comment:

2016

It will take fortitude to keep trying after disappointments, but you and I are made from some tough fabric.

_____ Like

Comment:

October 8

2011

Life is filled with so many twist n turns, but when u get on the right path, stay the course.

"The steps of a good man are ordered by the lord, n he delights n his way." Psalms 37:23

_____ Like

Comment:

Some people want to be left alone, honor their wishes.

_____ Like

Comment:

Sometimes u have to throw ur self a party. Dance as long as u want, Play ur own songs and enjoy ur self

Haven't done that in awhile. Sure was fun.

_____ Like

Comment:

2012

When I praise God, my atmosphere changes.

_____ Like

Comment:

2013

You get so much done when u are determined.

_____ Like

Comment:

2014

"He will reply, 'Truly I tell you, whatever you did not do for one of the least of these, you did not do for me.' Matthew 25:45

Help somebody today.

_____ Like

Comment:

October 9
2012
U can get back on track; it starts with believing u can, then do it.

_____ Like

Comment:

2013
If it weren't for obstacles, there would be no need to press.

_____ Like

Comment:

Who am I, that you would be mindful of me?

_____ Like

Comment:

This Sunday I will be ordained as a deacon at Restoring Life International Church 10 AM.

I'm excited!

_____ Like

Comment:

2015
When it comes to people, do they push you toward or away from your purpose?

_____ Like

Comment:

October 10
2011
After u figure out ur gift, would u mind sharing it with the world?
_____ Like
Comment:

2012
U know n I know there's a lot of places I could be, but there's no better place than the will of God.
_____ Like
Comment:

2013
Don't let anybody tell u that u can't do it or won't do it bc u can do it and u will do it.
_____ Like
Comment:

2014
The wisdom of God is in your worship to God.
_____ Like
Comment:

2015
Continue to study the word of God.
_____ Like
Comment:

2016
Nothing is going to stop you or me because of our faith.
_____ Like
Comment:

October 11
2011
It's not always about u; sometimes it's about the other people.
Today it's not all about me.
_____ Like
Comment:

2012
Look at you ready for the battle; it's already won you just have to show up.
_____ Like
Comment:

2013
What word will u speak over yourself today? Make it a powerful one.
_____ Like
Comment:

2016
It's a good thing that we are not frivolously using our credit cards.
_____ Like
Comment:

2017

When you look forward to the praise from people, be ready for the rejection from people too.

_____ Like

Comment:

October 12

2011

I'm not the same. God is changing me.

_____ Like

Comment:

2012

Thought provoking:

Last night our son told me in a whisper, "dad take a slow shower."

I'm still thinking about those words.

_____ Like

Comment:

Ur not always going to be "going through." One day you r going to be "going over."

_____ Like

Comment:

2016

There are great things going on behind the scenes in our favor, so rejoice.

_____ Like

Comment:

October 13
2011
Be a blessing.
Jesus always had folks messing with him, but it didn't stop him, and he never complained about it.
_____ Like
Comment:

October 14
2011
This can be a challenge.
A man's stomach shall be satisfied from the fruit of his mouth; From the produce of his lips, he shall be filled. Death and life are in the power of the tongue, And those who love it will eat its fruit. (Proverbs 18:20-21NKJV)
_____ Like
Comment:

2013
Ordination service was exciting, and I'm thrilled to be a deacon. Thank you all for your prayers and support, but my biggest weekend takeaway is going to the movies Saturday with my son watching "Cloudy with a Chance of Meatballs 2," he ate my food, we held hands, we were able to see the entire movies, then he asked to see it again.
_____ Like
Comment:

Don't settle. Get what u want out of life.
I wanted crab soup this evening, Pappas didn't have it, so I drove to Michael's and it's delicious.
_____ Like
Comment:

2016
You've done the hardest part; you got out the boat, now walk on water and ignore the winds.
_____ Like
Comment:

October 15
2011
Good day to get out n smell the cool breeze.
_____ Like
Comment:

When I am focused n organized the things I can do.
_____ Like
Comment:

2012
The thing u think u shouldn't do is probably what u should be doing.
_____ Like
Comment:

Stop being afraid.
_____ Like
Comment:

2013
U deserve everything u have and more.
_____ Like
Comment:

October 16
2012
Every time u get a thought about u that's not God's thoughts of u, please reject it.
_____ Like
Comment:

2013
U are really the bigger person when u learn to look over other people issues.
_____ Like
Comment:

2014
I'm really serious; God has been good to me.
I've been dancing all day because the joy of the Lord is my strength.
_____ Like
Comment:

2016

All I'm saying is, go about life with a made up mind.

_____ Like

Comment:

October 17

2011

U can do it. Don't let anybody tell u otherwise, including yourself.
Make it happen, captain.

_____ Like

Comment:

2012

U say, "forget about those past things." I say that's hard to do.
U promise me my future looks better than my past, well ok God.

_____ Like

Comment:

2013

I refrained from fast food the last pm. I saved money, but most of all I saved my body.

_____ Like

Comment:

2014

You're not that busy that you can't praise the Lord God.

_____ Like

Comment:

2016

You and I are replacing "I'll do it later" with "let me take care of that now."

_____ Like

Comment:

October 18

2011

Clean the bathroom first, then do the other work.

That's what I keep telling myself.

_____ Like

Comment:

2012

Lunch packed = money saved

_____ Like

Comment:

2013

For now u are reading n marveling over other people lives, but soon people are going to be marveling n reading about ur life.

_____ Like

Comment:

2016

Show the world your greatness, what are you waiting for?

_____ Like

Comment:

October 19
2012
It is not as it appears bc u walk by faith, not by sight. 2 Corin. 5:7
_____ Like
Comment:

2017
Stop wishing your past was different, instead, make your present and future greater.
_____ Like
Comment:

October 20
2011
God help me to trust u more.
_____ Like
Comment:

2014
The devil needs to know your habit of praying, reading the Word of God and walking in the power of God.
_____ Like
Comment:

October 21
2011

Some say, easier said than done.

If I never say it, i can be sure it will never be done.

Don't worry about what people think about u.

_____ Like

Comment:

October 22
2011

Just like u can't read their mind, u can't change it either.

Be secure.

_____ Like

Comment:

2012

Newness. New day, new mercy, new challenges, new opportunities, new relationships, new job, new money, new vision, new places, new friends, new books, new enemies, new levels, new devils, new greatness and new possibilities.

_____ Like

Comment:

2013

"Gravity" - A powerful movie about the human will, a must see.

_____ Like

Comment:

2015

What's keeping me from achieving, just me.

_____ Like

Comment:

2016

When I was a kid I use to be afraid to try this or that; now I can't wait to try this or that.

God will remove fear and give you his kind of faith to move mountains.

Embrace God today through a relationship with Jesus.

_____ Like

Comment:

2017

Isaiah 40:31King James Version (KJV)

31 But they that wait upon the Lord shall renew their strength; they shall mount up with wings as eagles; they shall run, and not be weary, and they shall walk, and not faint.

_____ Like

Comment:

October 23

2011

How can a person eat a medium pizza at 10 pm, but have a normal blood sugar at 8 am?

Must be nice.

_____ Like

Comment:

10 years married
10 years at my church
10th month
10 dollars in the bank
I'm rolling!
_____ Like
Comment:

Better to hang in there, than to hang out there.
_____ Like
Comment:

2012
U say, it's hard to eat right, exercise or stop smoking.
It's even harder to treat heart disease.
_____ Like
Comment:

2013
The rich man had his wealth that separated him from following Jesus, (Mark 10:21) what's separating you?
_____ Like
Comment:

2015

I don't think I'm bragging when I say, God has been good to me.

_____ Like

Comment:

2016

I don't think it's fair to serve an "on time God," but you show up late when it's time to serve.

_____ Like

Comment:

October 24
2011

I asked Coach Brown, why can't I win. He said, "u don't have a killer instinct to win." I told him I did want to win. He said, then why do u run behind the winners.

A killer instinct I learned was an overwhelming motivation to succeed. I caught on and I began to win.

Coach Brown those words will transcend to everything I do.

_____ Like

Comment:

Sometimes it can be scary, "But whoever listens to me will dwell safely, And will be secure, without fear of evil." (Proverbs 1:33 NKJV)

I like knowing that. I really do.

_____ Like

Comment:

2012

You have so much to do, no time for sin and foolishness.

_____ Like

Comment:

2013

Let ur children remember the quality time u gave them.

What will be ur legacy?

_____ Like

Comment:

2014

Pray.

_____ Like

Comment:

October 25
2011

U won't get a ticket to a live play. U won't go out to the movies, but u will allow OPD (other people's drama) to be acted out in front of you.

Cancel that show n see a real performance.

_____ Like

Comment:

2012

My family is close. Today I'm going to the movie with a sister n my brother. I can't wait.

_____ Like

Comment:

2013

I like reading a book I can immediately apply to my life.

_____ Like

Comment:

2015

God made me laugh today in church, when he let me know, "it's not that heavy."

_____ Like

Comment:

October 26

2011

Nothing like some indoor kickball to start the day.

_____ Like

Comment:

2012

Just left the doctors office. Got to take care of yourself.

_____ Like

Comment:

2015

If I wasn't working, I'd be at the library.

I hope my son Gosh learns this one lesson, never be afraid, for the Lord is with him, even when I can't be.

_____ Like

Comment:

2016

I'm going to do me today, you can join me and do you.

_____ Like

Comment:

2017

If you move or change your position due to being offended, you will remain unstable until you recover from the offense.

_____ Like

Comment:

October 27

2011

Lord empty me, then would u fill me.

_____ Like

Comment:

don't let people treat u bad.
U r better than that.
Have a standard of care and don't sway from it.
_____ Like
Comment:

2014
Prioritize.
_____ Like
Comment:

Receive unexpected goodness today
_____ Like
Comment:

October 28
2011
U might not be totally free, but at least ur not totally bound.
John 8:36
New International Version (NIV)
36 So if the Son sets you free, you will be free indeed.
_____ Like
Comment:

2013

Watch out for selfishness, instead replace it with giving.

_____ Like

Comment:

October 29

2011

4 things u can do with money

Save

Give

Self

Debt/Bill

...

Example if u had a dollar:

Save ____ cents

Give ____ cents

Self ____ cents

Debt/Bill ____ cents

_____ Like

Comment:

2012

The streets are so bare and it's so dark, where's the Light.

_____ Like

Comment:

2013

Ignorance will not dwell with u for long, soon u will pursue to know the truth.

_____ Like

Comment:

2015

I dare you to be different.

_____ Like

Comment:

2016

Our mission is possible because of the greater one in us.

_____ Like

Comment:

Be a good manager of your time, money and relationships, they pay huge dividends.

_____ Like

Comment:

2017

The enemy keeps fighting you and me, but we keep winning.

_____ Like

Comment:

October 30
2012
No cars on the road, but a walk in the rain is refreshing.

_____ Like

Comment:

2013
You are purpose driven and somethings on the road of ur life are noticeable, but not significant enough for you to stop and pay attention to.

_____ Like

Comment:

2015
Some people want to put you in a box.
They need to know that eagles soar.

_____ Like

Comment:

2016
When the financial increase comes, don't forget the kingdom of God.

_____ Like

Comment:

2017
Don't stop. Keep it moving.

_____ Like

Comment:

This GPS woman is pushy, lol.
_____ Like
Comment:

October 31
2011
U gonna get to ur dream, but it's gonna cost u something, don't be afraid to pay for it.
It's worth it.
_____ Like
Comment:

2012
It is by God's grace that I've been kept, not my own doings.
_____ Like
Comment:

2013
So many things to do, but I'll seek first the kingdom of God and his righteousness, then those things I got to do, there'll just be added to me.
Sounds like a good plan.
Matthew 6:33
_____ Like
Comment:

CHAPTER 11
November

November 1
2011
What if u discover that u have been preserved, n now u r about to be opened for the world to see.

Shine for God's glory.

_____ Like

Comment:

2012
Husbands and fathers, family is ur first ministry.

_____ Like

Comment:

2016
We are unbreakable.

_____ Like

Comment:

2017

The worst place you could be is outside the will of God, so the best place to be is right smack dab in the will of God.

_____ Like

Comment:

November 2

2012

3 am giving a bath, eating popsicles and playing football. I said, "family is ur first ministry."

_____ Like

Comment:

2016

We only have a season to make a difference, not a lifetime.

_____ Like

Comment:

November 3

2014

Are you whining or crying out to God, the response may be different?

_____ Like

Comment:

2016
Whatever that makes you come out of yourself to do, and someone is better off as a result of it, is walking in your purpose.
_____ Like
Comment:

November 4
2013
A kiss in the morning might wake her up, so I'll save it for later.
_____ Like
Comment:

2015
Nothing you say or do will stop me from fulfilling my dream.
Dreams come true because of efforts. Ecclesiastes 5:3
_____ Like
Comment:

2016
You know you're serious about debt reduction when you setup automatic payments to go to debtors.
_____ Like
Comment:

November 5
2011
U can't afford it. Get it later.

_____ Like

Comment:

2012
Finish what u started. You are not defeated.

_____ Like

Comment:

2013
Your enemies get to come to your celebration because God prepares your table in their presence.

_____ Like

Comment:

2015
There are some things for you to do and you can't shake the thoughts.

_____ Like

Comment:

2016

He came to his own people, and even they rejected him. John 1:11

Stop tripping about people who reject you, so was the case for Jesus.

But you got to read the next verse:

But to all who believed him and accepted him, he gave the right to become children of God. John 1:12

Now that's better.

_____ Like

Comment:

November 6

2011

Some people can't believe who u have become.

U r amazing them.

_____ Like

Comment:

There is a peace in trusting God.

_____ Like

Comment:

2012

It's not easy for you to get up and do what you do, but no this you are never alone.

_____ Like

Comment:

2013

Nobody is responsible for another person's feelings.

_____ Like

Comment:

It's just for a moment. It's not for a lifetime.

_____ Like

Comment:

I want the same thing you want, and that's the power of God.

_____ Like

Comment:

November 7
2011

Don't stand for an abusive relationship

Get help. Whoever u r.

_____ Like

Comment:

2012

Stay true to ur cause.

_____ Like

Comment:

2013

Be not bitter, but be better, bigger and bolder.

_____ Like

Comment:

2016

If you believe that strongly about it, then do it.

_____ Like

Comment:

November 8

2011

U say why pray. Why not pray.

Ever had a relationship were there was no communication? It didn't last, did it?

_____ Like

Comment:

2013

I love The Lord Jesus Christ.

_____ Like

Comment:

2016

You have a mind and a body, and you can't do what?

_____ Like

Comment:

2017

Have a heart filled with praise today.

_____ Like

Comment:

If you and I put in the time, it'll tell in the results.

_____ Like

Comment:

November 9

2011

U say, "the devil made me do it."

Naw u wanted to do it.

KIR (keep it real)

_____ Like

Comment:

2012

There was a time negativity dominated my thinking.

Today I make no apologies for positive posts.

Been there, done that, never to return.

_____ Like

Comment:

"Did I not tell you that if you believed you would see the glory of God." Jesus reminds Martha of his promise to raise Lazarus.

Didn't he promise you something too?

_____ Like

Comment:

November 10
2011

Ever had a day u were so excited that u danced in the rain?

Been there, done that.

_____ Like

Comment:

2015

Matthew 7:28-29 When Jesus had finished saying these things, the crowds were amazed at his teaching, because he taught as one who had authority, and not as their teachers of the law.

Whatever you do, do it with authority.

Don't be ordinary.

_____ Like

Comment:

2017

The cost of the anointing is expensive, but it's worth it.

_____ Like

Comment:

Say it and do it. That's the behavior of a non-procrastinator.

_____ Like

Comment:

November 11

2011

I'm still excited because a dream is coming true.

Would u get excited with me?

_____ Like

Comment:

2013

Momma used to drag me to church when I was young, but one day I went on my own and oh what a happy day!

_____ Like

Comment:

2015

Give folks a break today; nobody's perfect.

_____ Like

Comment:

2016

In life, a few will give you, but for the most part you and I will have to get it ourselves.

_____ Like

Comment:

Information is good, but information received is knowledge and knowledge applied appropriately is wisdom.

_____ Like

Comment:

November 12
2012

Car in shop for brake eval. I take the bus to work n two boxers charge me. The owner has to grab their chain to get them back in the yard.

"even though I walk through the valley of death, I will fear no evil, for you are with me." Psalms 23

_____ Like

Comment:

2013

It's not what you are going through, but the state of your attitude as you go through it.

_____ Like

Comment:

2016

One reason I desire to be closer to my God because I always want to be stronger than my enemies.

_____ Like

Comment:

November 13

2011

Make sure ur actions line up with ur words when u say, "I love you."

_____ Like

Comment:

2013

Use a timer to manage your time, and you will be surprised how much you accomplished.

No more wasting time.

_____ Like

Comment:

2014

If the Lord has told you to do it, why do you care what I think?

_____ Like

Comment:

2016

I could loudly complain or quietly change; it's my choice.

_____ Like

Comment:

November 14
2011
Remember the old karate movies; the good guy would get beaten, then he would learn a new fighting skill n beat his enemies.

What new style have u learned?

_____ Like

Comment:

2012
Washing dishes without gloves is so not cool.

_____ Like

Comment:

2013
Bills paid n I have enough left over for a sandwich. I'm not complaining. Lol

_____ Like

Comment:

November 15
2011
I heard these words for the first time 20 years ago; it's not what happens to u n life that matters as much as how u respond to what happens to u n life.

Lord help me to respond like u?

_____ Like

Comment:

U know that u r overcoming selfishness when u can rejoice about another person's success.

_____ Like

Comment:

2012

They say, "how do u do it."

You say, "for the Lord is my shepherd."

_____ Like

Comment:

2013

Your prayer life has a direct relationship to your personal life.

Be prayerful.

_____ Like

Comment:

2016

You and I might be the gossipers now, but later will be the gossiped.

Refrain from gossip. (a person who habitually reveals personal or sensational facts about others)

_____ Like

Comment:

When the money comes, will you know what to do with it?

_____ Like

Comment:

November 16
2011
Would u make a commitment to go to the House of God this Sunday?

_____ Like

Comment:

2012
14 But even if you should suffer for what is right, you are blessed. 1 Peter 3:14
Don't worry bout the naysayers.

_____ Like

Comment:

2016
I hesitated, pondered and questioned, then I just did it.

_____ Like

Comment:

2017
Do you give your word to God and sometimes renege?We all make promises to God and renege, forgive yourself and stay committed.

_____ Like

Comment:

Have a productive day, sweetheart .(Shawanda)

_____ Like

Comment:

November 17
2011
That's who u used to be n what u use to do.
_____ Like
Comment:

2015
I love you is the same as you I love.
_____ Like
Comment:

2016
You will spend a lifetime discovering who God is in the Bible and as a result, you will learn about yourself.
It's a book that is alive.
_____ Like
Comment:

November 18
2011
Don't get it twisted.
U r a success.
_____ Like
Comment:

2013

Stop hating on people. You are only going to help them reach their goal faster.

_____ Like

Comment:

2014

I believe that as a soldier of the Lord, you are not always to fight the enemy, but sometimes you are to rescue the lost and obtain the goods.

_____ Like

Comment:

I've been invited to play basketball in 20-degree weather with my son; sometimes you just have to say, yes.

_____ Like

Comment:

2016

Can you post anything else besides God posts? Yes I can, "Jesus saves."

_____ Like

Comment:

2017

You and I have a lot, but remember to get "wisdom" according to Proverbs 4:7.

_____ Like

Comment:

November 19
2012
Last week we were discussing potty training, this week private school vs public.
Boy, how time flys.
_____ Like
Comment:

2013
May I live most of what I post.
_____ Like
Comment:

2017
Guard your anointing. It has great potential.
_____ Like
Comment:

November 20
2012
Be strong and courageous today.
Your enemies are looking for an opportunity to attack.
_____ Like
Comment:

2013

Of all the places I would like to be, there's no better place than smack dab in the will of God!

_____ Like

Comment:

You are not going to have what they have because you are not going to do what they do.

_____ Like

Comment:

November 21

2011

If I would just believe n not doubt God will take care of the rest.

May we believe him the more.

_____ Like

Comment:

2012

I think I know why our son says; I have a "puter" n not a bed.

He just woke up n where was I, on the computer. Smh

_____ Like

Comment:

I'm at McDonald's this morning n the cashier is so, so friendly. I had to take a second look to see where I was.
I had to compliment this lady for being so, so friendly.
Be so, so friendly today.
_____ Like
Comment:

2013
Excellence is on my mind.
_____ Like
Comment:

2016
You can get a push to be better, but know one is going to drag you; you will have to take the initiative.
_____ Like
Comment:

November 22
2011
It's gonna get better u just wait n see.
"every day is not the same" Josephine Jordan
One of the wisest women to have lived.
_____ Like
Comment:

2012

Have a happy thanksgiving.

Enjoy the day with family n friends.

_____ Like

Comment:

2013

I'm a good steward of my body.

_____ Like

Comment:

2012

It doesn't matter what they say, just fulfill your assignment.

_____ Like

Comment:

November 23
2011

Stretch ur faith today.

_____ Like

Comment:

2012

Being determined n positive is the way.

U will have obstacles, but they r there to show ur strength.

_____ Like

Comment:

2016

When folks do you wrong, give them the unexpected response.

_____ Like

Comment:

Yesterday, I asked Goshen how much should I pay him for his allowance, and he stated the same price I had in mind.

The power of agreement.

_____ Like

Comment:

I believe God gives us quizzes and tests.

Pass the quiz and the test.

_____ Like

Comment:

November 24

2011

Invest n relationships; the return is high.

_____ Like

Comment:

Kryptonite made superman weak.

What's ur kryptonite?

We need u strong to save the day.

_____ Like

Comment:

2016

What's up?

_____ Like

Comment:

November 25

2011

U could have been picked for so many teams.

Aren't u glad u were picked for God's team?

U win!

_____ Like

Comment:

2013

Lord, I appreciate this new day, and I will make the most of it.

_____ Like

Comment:

November 26

2012

Ravens dug in for the win.

Word for today, "dig in."

_____ Like

Comment:

2013

Something good is about to happen for you because you are due.

_____ Like

Comment:

November 27
2012

Ur season is about to change. Flow with the move of the Spirit.

_____ Like

Comment:

2013

I'm so glad I don't do what I use to do.
Now that I know better, I will do better.

_____ Like

Comment:

Be able to discern when the season is over n that relationship n move on.

_____ Like

Comment:

November 28
2011

Be diligent today.

_____ Like

Comment:

2012

Get the estimates n second opinions before deciding on the matter.

After several estimates, now the auto work can be done. I have the peace.

_____ Like

Comment:

I'm not buying fast food tonight.

_____ Like

Comment:

2013

When u don't forgive, u hold urself in bondage mentally.

Learn to forgive and be thankful.

2016

The Bible is not the only book you should read, but it should be a daily book you read.

_____ Like

Comment:

November 29

2011

Rush rush rush. Slow down n say thanks for all he has done.

God's been good to u n me.

_____ Like

Comment:

2012

Be confident, not cocky.

Confident = humbly sure

Cocky = pridefully unsure

_____ Like

Comment:

2013

Don't expect any more or any less of yourself, you are doing your best.

_____ Like

Comment:

2016

When you see what's before you, govern yourself accordingly.

_____ Like

Comment:

November 30
2011

U say, " I would do it if."

I say, stop being afraid n do it.

_____ Like

Comment:

2012

The ways of the Lord are so much better than my ways.

Teach me your ways.

_____ Like

Comment:

2015

Only you, oh God, can satisfy my inner man.

_____ Like

Comment:

2016

There is so much more you, and I can do, if we continue to stay hungry and thirsty for success.

_____ Like

Comment:

CHAPTER 12
December

December 1
2012
When/if you fall dust urself off n run again

N don't go up n your head playing back the fall, people already have their copy of the video.

_____ Like

Comment:

2016
History can't be undone, but it can be made new.

_____ Like

Comment:

December 2
2011

but those who hope in the LORD will renew their strength. They will soar on wings like eagles; they will run and not grow weary, they will walk and not be faint. Isaiah 40:31(New International Version)
Think I'll fly today.
_____ Like
Comment:

Announcing the launch of my new business today:
Education for The Community, LLC
Education for The Community - provides educational lectures several times of the month to people in the community on drug addiction, HIV/AIDS, and mental illness.
new name www.mccraylectures.com
_____ Like
Comment:

2013

You are always making time for others, start making time for yourself.
_____ Like
Comment:

December 3
2012

Our preschooler sees the doctor.
Ouch!
Got to put together a bag of treats for him afterward.
_____ Like
Comment:

2013

A bright idea came to my mind and brought peace to me.

Be patient in the process.

_____ Like

Comment:

2016

It's a good day when you can give an account of your monies.

It's not how much you make, but how well you manage what you make.

Glad to be friends with "money making managers."

_____ Like

Comment:

December 4

2012

Thankful, that's what I'll be, thankful.

_____ Like

Comment:

2013

Be careful not to be distracted.

You have something to accomplish and it must be done.

_____ Like

Comment:

2016

That's how it is now, but who said it's going to stay that way.

_____ Like

Comment:

December 5
2011

Use to wonder why I was born eight years after my sister; then my father told me the plan he and my mom had.

I realize today; God knew me before I was in my mom's womb. Jeremiah 1:5

_____ Like

Comment:

Who said, you can't party at 10:30 am.

_____ Like

Comment:

Who said you couldn't have a party n your car with some Darwin Hobbs tunes.

_____ Like

Comment:

2012

It's my day, it's my turn, and it's on.

_____ Like

Comment:

Just left a business proposal for Education For The Community www.mccraylectures.com
Favor just isn't fair.
_____ Like
Comment:

What a birthday present God! — at White Marsh Movie Theatre.
_____ Like
Comment:

Well, this day is coming to a close, but boy did I enjoy myself.
First started in the presence of the God. People I'm telling you to want to be in the presence of God, not church, not a ministry but spending time with your God.
Next, I want to thank each and everyone who FB me, called, texted, email, sent a card or even thought about me today. Thank you, you didn't have to do it.
So all that's left for me to do is eat my butter pecan and think about the wonderful day I had.
_____ Like
Comment:

2013
Make the most of each day.
Your life is precious.
Had a wonderful birthday full of surprises, gifts, conversations, well wishes, and fun.
I come to realize you become more mature from your exposures.
Have wholesome exposures today.
_____ Like
Comment:

2014

Thank you, God for revealing your son Jesus to me, and afterward, I chose to follow after him.

_____ Like

Comment:

2015

Thank you all for your birthday well thoughts. I have enjoyed them all, and I hope I didn't miss thanking anyone.

I am thankful to be 50 and walking in my purpose.

I'm about to turn in as morning seems to come fast.

God Bless.

_____ Like

Comment:

December 6

December 7
2011
In Luke 18:41 Jesus asked the blind man, "what do you want me to do for you."
Ask me, Lord?
_____ Like
Comment:

2012
Don't be afraid to ask for help.
_____ Like
Comment:

2015
Trust in the Lord, not bc everything will be okay, but bc he knows what's best for you.
_____ Like
Comment:

December 8
2011
The dream must come to pass.
_____ Like
Comment:

December 9
2011
Never compromise what you know to be right bc of a people phobia
Been there, done that, but I've grown.

_____ Like

Comment:

2013
Are you going to believe God or what?

_____ Like

Comment:

2016
I refuse to be afraid anymore.

_____ Like

Comment:

December 10
2012
Step out there with me.
The water may be cold n deep, but don't be afraid.

_____ Like

Comment:

2013

I'm planning to be successful.

I'm writing my plans on the calendar, blackboard and entering them in the phone.

I won't fail bc I planned.

_____ Like

Comment:

2015

You can outrun your past if you turn your head around.

_____ Like

Comment:

December 11

2012

I take refuge in the Lord Jesus.

If you are ashamed of him. He will be ashamed of you when he comes. Luke 9:26

_____ Like

Comment:

2013

Don't go comparing your life to others.

You don't know what they had to do to get what they have.

_____ Like

Comment:

2016
You can partially trust a man, but you can totally trust God.
_____ Like
Comment:

December 12
2011
Family fellowship, fun, and food this week. Yum, yum yum
_____ Like
Comment:

2012
Be extra kind today; somebody needs it.
_____ Like
Comment:

2013
Silence is okay.
Who told you that you had to comment on everything people say?
v

2014
I keep praying because I like the changes.
Prayer changes things.
_____ Like
Comment:

December 13
2011
My son said to me in the car, "God is great, Amen."
That's the word for me today.
_____ Like
Comment:

2012
Have a great day. You say how because you say so.
_____ Like
Comment:

There's so much power in your tongue.
_____ Like
Comment:

2013
"Never be so busy that you don't have time for people."
From a former patient in 1986.
_____ Like
Comment:

2016
Sometimes we are afraid to try because we say, "what if I fail?"
What if you get up?
_____ Like
Comment:

December 14
2011
Gave my son his toothbrush n he said, "thank u so much."
That's my word for today.
So much will I be thankful for?
_____ Like
Comment:

2012
Aren't u glad that, "what u see is what u get."
No more double living.
_____ Like
Comment:

2016
It's not what I want to do; it's what I got to do.
_____ Like
Comment:

December 15
2011
No words out of the babe, just a hug to the leg.
May I always have more time than money for him.
_____ Like
Comment:

2016

Your alarm clock is for more than waking you up for work, school or volunteering.

_____ Like

Comment:

December 16

2011

Nothing like some hand clapping, key jingling, dancing with the babe.

_____ Like

Comment:

2013

If your tv could be paused for a week, then you would have time to get it done.

_____ Like

Comment:

2015

Only the strong will thrive.

_____ Like

Comment:

2016

Some debt is not your friend, so stop hanging out with him.

Instead, "do not forsake wisdom, and she will protect you; love her, and she will watch over you." Proverbs 4:6

_____ Like

Comment:

December 17
2012
Life is precious.

Enjoy yours n love others.

_____ Like

Comment:

2013
Don't be distracted by yesterday's events.

Today is a new day.

_____ Like

Comment:

December 18
2011
Enjoy this beautiful day. You and your beautiful spirit.

_____ Like

Comment:

2013
just had a joy comes in the morning moment.

_____ Like

Comment:

2015

Painting action figures on a Friday night with our son.

_____ Like

Comment:

December 19
2011

So I press, knowing that I am not alone.

If God is for me, then who can be against me. Romans 8:31

_____ Like

Comment:

2012

Deposited a check from home to the bank, that's cool.

Technology is amazing.

_____ Like

Comment:

2013

It doesn't matter how late you stay up or how early you get up, but know this you got to get it done.

_____ Like

Comment:

2017

You want what's good, but God wants to give you what's best.

_____ Like

Comment:

December 20

2011

How would you react to a new job, a new car, a new appliance, a new baby, a new home or a new relationship?

What about a new day that you have never seen before?

_____ Like

Comment:

2012

Joy, love n peace.

Oh if we had more, try to spread some today.

_____ Like

Comment:

2013

I'm thankful for the place I'm in, no longer trying to figure it out.

_____ Like

Comment:

2015
Believers must practice love and forgiveness.
_____ Like
Comment:

2016
It may be a repeat of the same, but repetitions can bring great results, look at the weightlifter.
_____ Like
Comment:

I want to see you complete your book next year, so if you are serious, inbox me your email address, and I will share some "trade secrets" to help you.
_____ Like
Comment:

December 21
2011
Once upon a time, when I ran summer track. I ask coach Marilyn Bevans what did she think of my performance?
She said, "u performed as well as u practiced."
Don't look for an A when you are making C effort.
_____ Like
Comment:

Don't get symptoms confused with the condition. This _____ is just a symptom of a condition. Once you get the condition in check, the symptoms go away.
_____ Like
Comment:

2012
You are so positive.
I shouldn't be surprised, look at who you are connected to.
_____ Like
Comment:

December 22
2011
Those of you who wanted to go to California for Christmas, you can save your money n stay here.
_____ Like
Comment:

2015
Never be ashamed of the name, for there is power in the name of Jesus.
_____ Like
Comment:

If you send Jesus a friend request, he will always accept.
_____ Like
Comment:

2016

Thank God, that you are not lazy.

_____ Like

Comment:

December 23
2011

Trying to shop on an empty stomach not good, thanks, McD's for a scrumptious Cinnamon Melt.

_____ Like

Comment:

December 24
2012

Good family, fellowship, food, and fun.

Glad to see a member I haven't seen in awhile at family outings.

You need your family.

_____ Like

Comment:

2013

You were created for fellowship.

Spread the love.

_____ Like

Comment:

December 25
2013
I had a wonderful family time of fellowship this holiday, hope you did too.

_____ Like

Comment:

December 26
2012
For some of us, if u want to be reminded of your physical freedom see, "Django."
But if you want a reminder of your spiritual freedom, see "Jesus."

_____ Like

Comment:

2015
If you are wondering what to keep or throw away if you have to think more than two seconds on an item, throw it away.

_____ Like

Comment:

2016
You and I know what we need to do and we can start now!

_____ Like

Comment:

December 27
2011
Purpose to be what God has already ordained you to be.

_____ Like

Comment:

2013
It's better to do it, then to say you are going to do it.
You only get credit for what's done.

_____ Like

Comment:

December 28
2010
Would he still be your God, even if things were not going right?

_____ Like

Comment:

2011
Being healthy is not so people can tell you how good you look, but your heart, brain, lungs n bones need to tell you how good they feel.
Don't wait until the 1st to get healthy. Make it a lifelong venture.

_____ Like

Comment:

2016

All the good you do behind the scenes is about to be displayed.

_____ Like

Comment:

December 29

2010

Just thought, when you like the service at a restaurant you give a financial tip but what about telling the person they did a good job. It is said words are powerful. For now on that's what I'll do give a verbal tip positive or negative.

_____ Like

Comment:

2011

What else must God do to prove his love to you?

John 3:16

_____ Like

Comment:

2012

No rain, no snow, no fear can stop me bc I'm "Pushing On."

_____ Like

Comment:

2016

Do it anyway, despite the "likes."

_____ Like

Comment:

December 30

2011

Should I fight this battle and will I win?

That's the question.

1 Samuel 30:8

_____ Like

Comment:

2013

You ever had a time when you did not know what to say; those were times when silence was golden.

_____ Like

Comment:

2014

Prayerful people = Powerful people

_____ Like

Comment:

2016
Spend your time wisely; you are not able to get refunds.
_____ Like
Comment:

December 31
2013
My prayer for you and me is that we come to understand the power of our will.
_____ Like
Comment:

2014
I was on my way to destruction; then God saved me.
Oh hallelujah!
_____ Like
Comment:

good leader = good follower
_____ Like
Comment:

2015
God wants your faithfulness, not your "fakefulnes."
_____ Like
Comment:

2016

You're not going to be the same next year. You might have to change your name.

_____ Like

Comment:

Made in the USA
Columbia, SC
26 February 2018